Y0-CVG-184

With the Compliments of
SUN YAT-SEN'S LIB
11-A Chung Shan Rd. (S)
Taipei, Taiwan
China

The International Development of China

By
Sun Yat-sen

With 16 Maps in the Text and a Folding Map at end

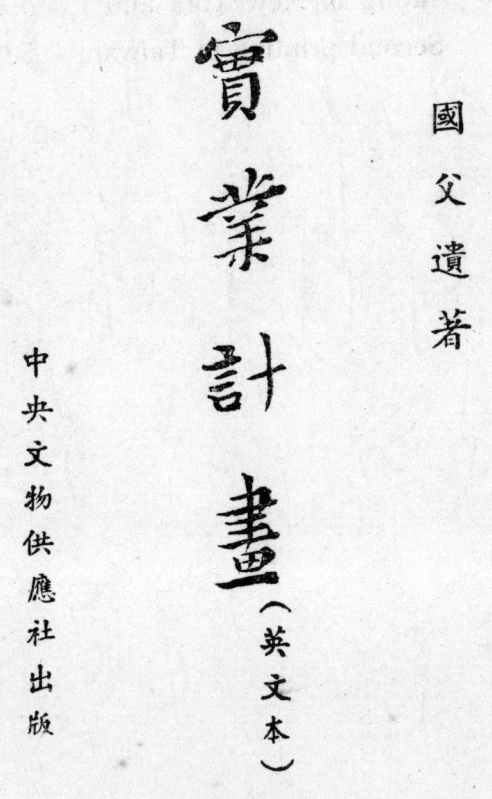

實業計畫（英文本）

國父遺著

中央文物供應社出版

Published by
CHINA CULTURAL SERVICE
Taipei, Taiwan

First printing in New York and London, 1922.
Second printing in Taiwan, 1953.

Printed by
Sino-American Publishing Co., Ltd.
TAIPEI, TAIWAN
1953

This work is
affectionately dedicated
to
SIR JAMES AND LADY CANTLIE
My revered teacher and devoted friends
to whom I once owed my life

PREFACE

As soon as Armistice was declared in the recent World War, I began to take up the study of the International Development of China, and to form programs accordingly. I was prompted to do so by the desire to contribute my humble part in the realization of world peace. China, a country possessing a territory of 4,289,000 square miles, a population of 400,000,000 people, and the richest mineral and agricultural resources in the world, is now a prey of militaristic and capitalistic powers—a greater bone of contention than the Balkan Peninsula. Unless the Chinese question can be settled peacefully, another world war greater and more terrible than the one just past will be inevitable. In order to solve the Chinese question. I suggest that the vast resources of China be developed internationally under a socialistic scheme, for the good of the world in general and the Chinese people in particular. It is my hope that as a result of this, the present spheres of influence can be abolished; the international commercial war can be done away with; the internecine capitalistic competition can be got rid of, and last, but not least, the class struggle between capital and labor can be avoided. Thus the root of war will be forever exterminated so far as China is concerned.

Each part of the different programs in this International Scheme, is but a rough sketch or a general policy produced from a layman's thought with very limited materials at his disposal. So alterations and changes will have to be made after scientific investigation and detailed survey. For instance, in regard to the projected Great Northern Port, which is to be situated between the mouths of the Tsingho and the Lwanho, the writer thought that the entrance of the harbor should be at the eastern side of the port but from actual survey by technical engineers, it is found that the entrance of the harbor should be at the western side of the port instead. So I crave great indulgence on the part of experts and specialists.

I wish to thank Dr. Monlin Chiang, Mr. David Yui, Dr. Y. Y. Tsu, Mr. T. Z. Koo, and Dr. John Y. Lee, who have given me great assistance in reading over the manuscripts with me.

SUN YAT-SEN.

CANTON, April 25, 1921.

INTRODUCTION

After World War I, Dr. Sun Yat-sen suggested a plan for international development of China, in which he set forth clearly before the world the idea that international cooperation in the development of China's vast resources was far more profitable for world prosperity than international rivalry in exploitation of that vast underdeveloped country.

More than thirty years have elapsed and great changes in the world situation have taken place since this volume was published in 1922, yet his words are ringing true in the present day world affairs.

Dr. Sun Yat-sen's ideas on international development of China find their counterparts at the present day in President Eisenhower's recent speech on world aid and reconstruction as a solution to the world problem.

In answering to the recent peace offensive of Soviet Russia after Stalin's death, President Eisenhower declared that all nation should join "in devoting a substantial percentage of any savings achieved by real disarmament to a fund for world aid and reconstruction . . . We are ready, in short, to dedicate our strength to serving needs, rather than fears, of the world."

The views expressed by President Eisenhower were wider in scope than the ideas behind the Marshal Plan and still much wider than those behind the Consortium created after World War I, yet the spirit behind them was one and the same.

Here a few words about the Consortium may be required to refresh our memory. The Consortium was formed in Paris for the purpose of assisting China in developing her natural resources. This was the first attempt by the American government to launch a constructive program by international cooperation in the development of China.

Dr. Sun Yat-sen had high hopes for the Consortium for he said that since it was initiated by the American government, "we need not fear the lack of capital to start work in our industrial development."

At the same time he entertained legitimate fears that the plan might be upset by the Japanese militarists who "still think that war is the most profitable national pursuit and their General Staff keeps on planning a war once in a decade."

Subsequent events proved that he was right.

The Consortium was clipped in the bud by international rivalry, instigated by the Japanese military clique whcih wanted nothing of the sort to be put in effect in the development of Manchuria. What Japan wanted was the so-called "co-prosperity in Greater Asia" in exclusion of economic interests of the West, especially the United States.

In a short span of some ten years a series of incidents created by the Japanese militarists led eventually to a greater one known as the "Mukden Incident" in 1931. It was soon followed by Marco Polo Bridge in 1937 which sparked a total war in the Far East.

At Pearl Harbor the two regional wars were merged into one great World War.

After World War II, international economic cooperation took the form first of the UNRRA and then of the Marshal Plan which were world-wide aid to rehabilitate and reconstruct the vast devastated areas of the world. From the aid substantial benefits have accrued to the recipient countries.

Likewise in Taiwan, economic cooperation between the United States and Free China has not only rehabilitated the industries damaged during the war, but made great improvement on both industry and agriculture. Good results of international cooperation were here clearly shown.

As for economic policy in China, Dr. Sun Yat-sen tried to strike a balance between private enterprise and state industry. "All matters that can be and better carried out by private enterprise should be left to private hands which should be encouraged and fully protected by liberal laws," and "that cannot be taken up by private concerns and those that possess monopolistic character should be taken up as national (state) undertakings."

This economic policy is held as a guiding principle for Free China today.

Thus Dr. Sun Yat-sen envisioned a plan by which capitalism is to work together hand in hand with socialism in one and the same country. "In a nutshell," said he, "it is my idea to make capitalism create socialism in China so that these two economic forces of human evolution will work side by side in future civilization."

The ideas of Dr. Sun Yat-sen were much more than a historical interest. The problems presented in this volume are living problems of the world today. And, therefore, there are ample reasons for its reprint.

Chiang Monlin

Taiwan (Formosa), May 1953.

CONTENTS

	PAGE
PREFACE	V
INTRODUCTION	VII
THE INTERNATIONAL DEVELOPMENT OF CHINA	1
PROGRAM I	9
PROGRAM II	27
PROGRAM III	69
PROGRAM IV	115
PROGRAM V	173
PROGRAM VI	195
CONCLUSION	203
APPENDIX I	209
APPENDIX II	220
APPENDIX III	225
APPENDIX IV	227
APPENDIX V	228
APPENDIX VI	230

MAPS

	FACING PAGE
FIGURE 1	14
FIGURE 2	15
MAP I	16
MAP II	17
MAP III	30
MAP IV	31
MAP V	40
MAP VI	41
MAP VII	44
MAP VIII	45
MAP IX	48
MAP X	49
MAP XI	74
MAP XII	75
MAP XIII	76
MAP XIV	77
MAP XV	84
MAP XVI	85

MAP AT END

THE INTERNATIONAL DEVELOPMENT OF CHINA

A Project to Assist the Readjustment of Post-Bellum Industries

It is estimated that during the last year of the World War the daily expenses of the various fighting nations amounted to two hundred and forty millions of dollars gold. It is accepted by even the most conservative, that only one half of this sum was spent on munitions and other direct war supplies, that is, one hundred and twenty millions of dollars gold. Let us consider these war supplies from a commercial point of view. The battlefield is the market for these new industries, the consumers of which are the soldiers. Various industries had to be enlisted and many new ones created for the supplies. In order to increase the production of these war commodities day by day, people of the warring countries and even those of the neutral states had to be content with the barest necessities of life and had to give up all former comforts and luxuries.

Now the war is ended and the sole market of these war supplies has closed, let us hope, forever, for the good of humanity. So, from now on we are concerned with the problem as to how a readjustment may be brought about. What must be considered first is the reconstruction of the various countries, and next the supply of comforts and luxuries that will have to be resumed. We remember that one hundred and twenty million dollars were spent every day on direct war supplies. Let us then suppose that the two items mentioned will take up one half of this sum, that is, sixty millions of dollars a day which will still leave us a balance of sixty million dollars a day. Besides, the many millions of soldiers who were once consumers will from now on become producers again. Furthermore, the unification and nationalization of all the industries, which I might call the Second Industrial Revolution, will be more far-reaching than that of the first one in which Manual Labor was displaced by Machinery. This second industrial revolution will increase the productive power of man many times more than the first one. Consequently, this unification of industries on account of the World War will further complicate the readjustment of the post-war industries. Just imagine sixty million dollars a day or twenty-one billions and nine hundred millions of dollars a year of new trade created by the war suddenly have to stop when peace is concluded! Where in this world can Europe and America look for a market to consume this enormous saving from the war?

If the billions of dollars worth of war industries can find no place in the post-bellum readjustment, then they will be a pure economic waste. The result will not only disturb the economic condition of the producing countries, but will also be a great loss to the world at large.

All the commercial nations are looking to China as the only "dumping ground" for their over-production. The prewar condition of trade was unfavorable to China. The balance of imports over exports was something over one hundred million dollars gold annually. The market of China under this condition could not expand much for soon after there will be no more money or commodities left for exchanging goods with foreign countries. Fortunately, the natural resources of China are great and their proper development would create an unlimited market for the whole world and would utilize the greater part, if not all of the billions of dollars worth of war industries soon to be turned into peace industries.

China is the land that still employs manual labor for production and has not yet entered the first stage of industrial evolution, while in Europe and America the second stage is already reached. So China has to begin the two stages of industrial evolution at once by adopting the machinery as well as the nationalization of production. In this case China will require machinery for her vast agriculture, machinery for her rich mines, machinery for the building of her innumerable factories, machinery for her extensive transportation system and machinery for all her public utilities. Let us see how this new demand for machinery will help in the readjustment of war industries. The workshops that turn out cannon can easily be made to turn out steam rollers for the construction of roads in China. The workshops that turn out tanks can be made to turn out trucks for the transportation of the raw materials that are lying everywhere in China. And all sorts of warring machinery can be converted into peaceful tools for the general development of China's latent wealth. The Chinese people will welcome the development of our country's resources provided that it can be kept out of Mandarin corruption and ensure the mutual benefit of China and of the countries cooperating with us.

It might be feared by some people in Europe and

America that the development of China by war machinery, war organization and technical experts might create unfavorable competitiont o foreign industries. I, therefore, propose a scheme to develop a new market in China big enough both for her own products and for products from foreign countries. The scheme will be along the following lines:

I. The Development of a Communications System.

    (a) 100,000 miles of railways.
    (b) 1,000,000 miles of macadam roads.
    (c) Improvement of existing canals.
        (1) Hangchow-Tientsin canals.
        (2) Sikiang-Yangtze canals.
    (d) Construction of new canals.
        (1) Liaoho-Sunghwakiang canal.
        (2) Others to be projected.
    (e) River conservancy.
        (1) To regulate the embankments and channel of the Yangtze River from Hankow to the sea thus facilitating ocean-going ships to reach that port at all seasons.
        (2) To regulate the Hoangho embankments and channel to prevent floods.
        (3) To regulate the Sikiang.
        (4) To regulate the Hwaiho.
        (5) To regulate various other rivers.

(f) The construction of more telegraph lines and telephone and wireless systems all over the country.

II. The Development of Commercial Harbors.

(a) Three largest ocean ports with future capacity equalling New York harbor to be constructed in North, Central and South China.

(b) Various smal commercial and fishing harbors to be constructed along the coast.

(c) Commercial docks to be constructed along all navigable rivers.

III. Modern Cities with Public Utilities to be Constructed in All Railway Centers, Termini and alongside Harbors.

IV. Water Power Development.

V. Iron and Steel Works and Cement Works on the Largest Scale in Order to Supply the Above Needs.

VI. Mineral Development.

VII. Agricultural Development.

VIII. Irrigational Work on the Largest Scale in Mongolia and Sinkiang.

IX. Reforestation in Central and North China.

X. Colonization in Manchuria, Mongolia, Sinkiang, Kokonor, and Tibet.

If the above program could be carried out gradually, China will not only be the "Dumping Ground" for foreign goods but actually will be the "Economic Ocean" capable of absorbing all the surplus capital as quickly as the Industrial Nations can possibly produce by the coming Industrial Revolution of Nationalized Productive Machinery. Then there will be no more competition and commercial struggles in China as well as in the world.

The recent World War has proved to Mankind that war is ruinous to both the Conqueror and the Conquered, and worse for the Aggressor. What is true in military warfare is more so in trade warfare. Since President Wilson has proposed a League of Nations to end military war in the future, I desire to propose to end the trade war by cooperation and mutual help in the Development of China. This will root out probably the greatest cause of future wars.

The world has been greatly benefited by the development of America as an industrial and a commercial Nation. So a developed China with her four hundred millions of population, will be another New World in the economic sense. The nations which will take part in this development will reap immense advantages. Furthermore, international cooperation of this kind cannot but help to strengthen the Brotherhood of Man. Ultimately, I am sure, this will culminate to be the keystone in the arch of the League of Nations.

In order to carry out this project successfully I suggest that three necessary steps must be taken: First, that the various Governments of the Capital-supplying Powers must agree to joint action and a unified policy to form an International Organization with their war work organizers, administrators and experts of various lines to formulate plans and to standardize materials in order to prevent waste and to facilitate work. Second, the confidence of the Chinese people must be secured in order to gain their cooperation and enthusiastic support. If the above two steps are accomplished, then the third step is to open formal negotiation for the final contract of the project with the Chinese Government. For which I suggest that it be on the same basis as the contract I once concluded with the Pauling Company of London, for the construction of the Canton-Chungking Railway, since it was the fairest to both parties and the one most welcomed by the Chinese people, of all contracts that were ever made between China and the foreign countries.

And last but not least, a warning must be given that mistakes such as the notorious Sheng Shun Hwai's nationalized Railway Scheme in 1911 must not be committed again. In those days foreign bankers entirely disregarded the will of the Chinese people, and thought that they could do everything with the Chinese Government alone. But to their regret, they found that the contracts which they had concluded with the Government, by heavy bribery, were only to be blocked by the people later on. Had the foreign bankers gone in the right way of first securing the confidence of the Chinese people, and then approaching the Government for a contract, many things might have been accomplished without a hitch. Therefore, in this International Project we must pay more attention to the people's will than ever before.

If my proposition is acceptable to the Capital-supplying Powers, I will furnish further details.

PROGRAM I

The industrial development of China should be carried out along two lines: (1) by private enterprise and (2) by national undertaking. All matters that can be and are better carried out by private enterprise should be left to private hands which should be encouraged and fully protected by liberal laws. And in order to facilitate the industrial development by private enterprise in China, the hitherto suicidal internal taxes must be abolished, the cumbersome currency must be reformed, the various kinds of official obstacles must be removed, and transportation facilities must be provided. All matters that cannot be taken up by private concerns and those that possess monopolistic character should be taken up as national undertakings. It is for this latter line of development that we are here endeavoring to deal with. In this national undertaking, foreign capital have to be invited, foreign experts and organizers have to be enlisted, and gigantic methods have to be adopted. The property thus created will be state owned and will be managed for the benefit of the whole nation. During the construction and the operation of each of these national undertakings, before its capital and interest are fully repaid, it will be managed and supervised by foreign experts under Chinese employment. As one of their obligations, these foreign experts have to undertake the training of Chinese assistants to take their places in the future. When the capital and interest of each undertaking are paid off, the Chinese Government will have the option to employ either foreigners or Chinese to manage the concern as it thinks fit.

Before entering into the details of this International Development Scheme, four principles have to be considered:

(1) The most remunerative field must be selected in order to attract foreign capital.

(2) The most urgent needs of the nation must be met.

(3) The lines of least resistance must be followed.

(4) The most suitable positions must be chosen.

In conformity with the above principles, I formulate PROGRAM I as follows:

I. The construction of a great Northern Port on the Gulf of Pechili.

II. The building of a system of railways from the Great Northern Port to the Northwestern extremity of China.

III. The Colonization of Mongolia and Sinkiang (Chinese Turkestan).

IV. The construction of canals to connect the inland waterway systems of North and Central China with the Great Northern Port.

V. The development of the iron and coal fields in Shansi and the construction of an iron and steel works.

These five projects will be worked out as one program, for each of them will assist and accelerate the development of the others. The Great Northern Port will serve as a base of operation of this International Development Scheme, as well as a connecting link of transportation and communication between China and the outer world. The other four projects will be centered around it.

PART I

THE GREAT NORTHERN POINT

I propose that a great deep water and ice free port be constructed on the Gulf of Pechili. The need of such a port in that part of China has been keenly felt for a long time. Several projects have been proposed such as the deepening of the Taku Bar, the construction of a harbor in the Chiho estuary, the Chinwangtao Harbor which has actually been carried out on a small scale and the Hulutao Harbor which is on the point of being constructed. But the site of my projected port is in none of these places for the first two are too far from the deep water line and too near to fresh water which freezes in winter. So it is impossible to make them into deep water and ice free ports, while the last two are too far away from the center of population and are unprofitable as commercial ports. The locality of my projected port is just at midway between Taku and Chinwangtao and at a point between the mouths of the Tsingho and Lwanho, on the cape of the coast line between Taku and Chinwangtao. This is one of the points nearest to deep water in this Gulf. With the fresh water of the Tsingho and Lwanho diverted away, it can be made a deep water and ice free port without much difficulty. Its distance to Tientsin is about seventy or eighty miles less than that of Chinwangtao to Tientsin. Moreover, this port can be connected with the inland waterway systems of North and

Central China by canal, whereas in the case of Chinwangtao and Hulutao this could not be done. So this port is far superior as a commercial harbor than Hulutao or Chinwangtao which at present is the only ice free port in the Gulf of Pechili.

From a commercial standpoint this port will be a paying proposition from the very beginning of its construction, owing to the fact that it is situated at the center of the greatest salt industry in China. The cheapest salt is produced here by sun evaporation only. If modern methods could be added, also utilizing the cheap coal near by, the production could increase many times more and the cost could thus be made cheaper. Then it can supply the whole of China with much cheaper salt. By this industry alone it is quite sufficient to support a moderate sized harbor which must be the first step of this great project. Besides, there is in the immediate neighborhood the greatest coal mine that has yet been developed in China, the Kailan Mining Company. The output of its colliery is about four million tons a year. At present the company uses its own harbor, Chinwanytao, for shipping its exports. But our projected port is much nearer to its colliery than Chinwangtao. It can be connected with the mine by canal thus providing it with a much cheaper carriage than by rail to Chinwangtao. Furthermore, our projected port will in future consume much of the Kailan coal. Thus eventually the Company must use our port as a shipping stage for its exports. Tientsin, the largest commercial center in North China, has no deep harbor and is ice bound several months a year in winter, and so has to use our projected port entirely as an outlet for its world trade. This is the local need only but for this alone it is quite sufficient to make our projected port a paying proposition.

But my idea is to develop this port as large as New York in a reasonable limit of time. Now, let us survey the hinterland to see whether the possibility justifies my ideal or not. To the southwest are the provinces of Chili and Shansi, and the Hoangho valley with a population of nearly a hundred millions. To the northwest are the undeveloped Jehol district and the vast Mongolian Prairie with their virgin soil waiting for development, Chili with its dense population and Shansi with its rich mineral resources have to depend upon this port as their only outlet to the sea. And if the future Dolon Nor and Urga Railway is completed with connection to the Siberian line then Central Siberia will also have to use this as its nearest seaport. Thus its contributing or rather distributing area will be larger than that of New York. Finally, this port will become the true terminus of the future Eurasian Railway System, which will connect the two continents. The land which we select to be the site of our projected port is now almost worth next to nothing. Let us say two or three hundred square miles be taken up as national property absolutely for our future city building. If within forty years we could develop a city as large as Philadelphia, not to say New York, the land value alone will be sufficient to pay off the capital invested in its development.

The need of such a port in this part of China goes without saying. For the provinces of Chili, Shansi, Western Shantung, Northern Honan, a part of Fengtien and the greater part of Shensi and Kansu with a population of about

100 millions are lacking of a seaport of this kind. Mongolia and Sinkiang as well as the rich coal and iron fields of Shansi will also have to depend on the Chili coast as their only outlet to the sea. And the millions of congested population of the coast and the Yangtze valley need an entrance to the virgin soil of the Mongolian Prairie and the Tienshan Valley. The port will be the shortest doorway and the cheapest passage to these regions.

The locality of our projected port is nearest to deep water line, and far away from any large river which might carry silt to fill up the approach of the harbor like those of the Hoangho entrance and the Yangtze estuary which cause great trouble to conservancy work. So it has no great natural obstacle to be overcome. Moreover, it is situated in an arid plain with few people living on it, so it has no artificial hindrance to be overcome. We can do whatever we please in the process of construction.

As regards the planning and estimation of the work of the harbor construction and city building, I must leave them to experts who have to make extensive surveys and soundings before detailed plan and proper estimation could be made. Whereas for rough reference see Map I, and figures 1 and 2.*

> As soon as this first program reached the American Legation in Peking, the former Minister, Dr. Paul S. Reinsch, immediately sent an expert to survey the site which the writer indicated, and found that it is really the best site on the Chili Coast for a world harbor, excepting that the entrance of the port should be at the west side instead of the east side as the writer proposed. Detailed plans have been made as figures 1 and 2.

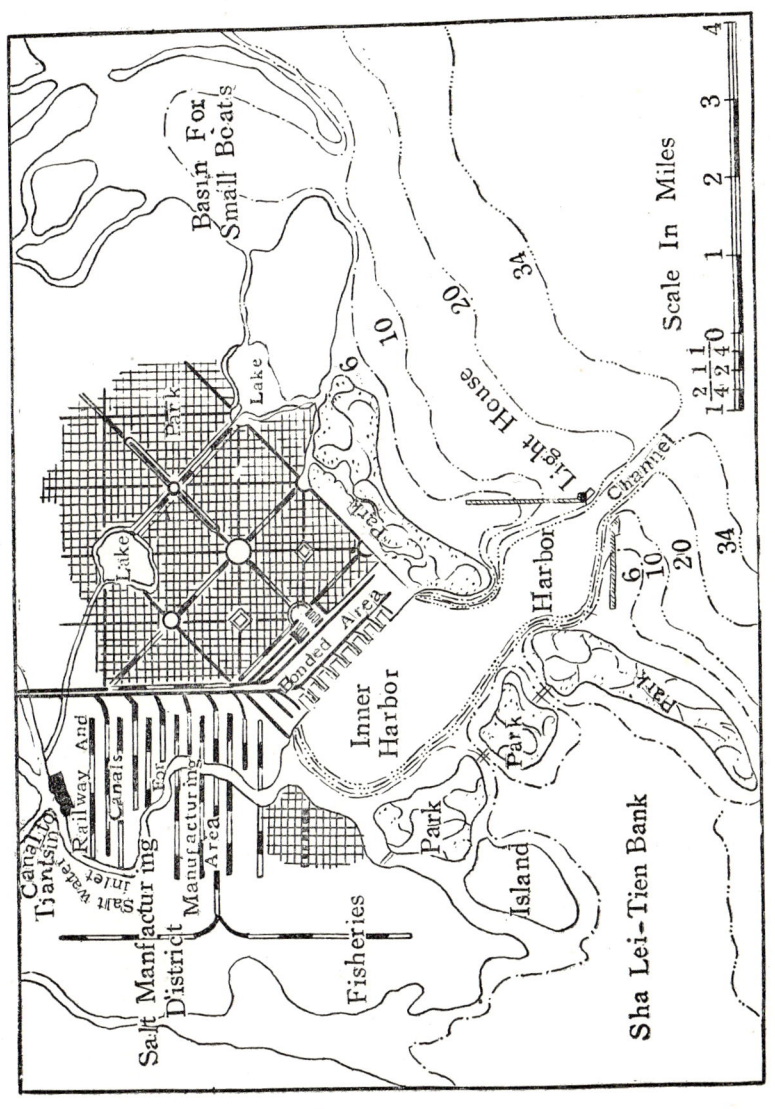

FIGURE 1

FIGURE 2

PART II

The Northwest Railway System

Our projected Railway will start at the Great Northern Port and follow the Lwan Valley to the prairie city of Dolon Nor, a distance of three hundred miles. This railway should be built in double tracks at the commencement. As our projected Port is a starting point to the sea, so Dolon Nor is a gate to the vast prairie which our projected Railway System is going to tap. It is from Dolon Nor our Northwestern Railway System is going to radiate. First, a line N. N. E. will run parallel to the Khingan Range to Khailar, and thence to Moho, the gold district on the right bank of the Amur River. This line is about eight hundred miles in length. Second, a line N. N. W. to Kurelun, and thence to the frontier to join the Siberian line near Chita. This line has a distance of about six hundred miles. Third, a trunk line northwest, west, and southwest, skirting off the northern edge of the desert proper, to Urumochi at the western end of China, a distance of about one thousand six hundred miles all on level land. Fourth, a line from Urumochi westward to Ili, a distance of about four hundred miles. Fifth, a line from Urumochi southeast across the Tienshan gap into the Darim basin, then turning southwest running along the fertile zone between the southern watershed of the Tienshan and the northern edge of the Darim Desert, to Kashgar, and thence turning southeast to another fertile zone between the eastern watershed of the Pamir, the northern watershed of the Kuenlum Mountain and the southern edge of the Darim Desert, to the city of Iden or Keria, a distance of about one thousand two hundred miles all on level land. Sixth, a branch from the Dolon Nor Urumochi Trunk Line, which I shall call Junction A, to Urga and thence to the frontier city Kiakata, a distance of about three hundred and fifty miles. Seventh, a branch from Junction B to Uliassutai and beyond N. N. W. up to the frontier, a distance of about six hundred miles. And eighth, a branch from Junction C northwest to the frontier, a distance of about four hundred and fifty miles. See Map II.

Regarded from the principle of "following the line of least resistance" our projected railways in this program is the most ideal one. For most of the seven thousand miles of lines under this project are on perfectly level land. For instance, the Trunk Line from Dolon Nor to Kashgar and beyond, about a distance of three thousand miles right along is on the most fertile plain and encounters no natural obstacles, neither high mountains nor great rivers.

Regarded from the principle of "the most suitable position," our projected railways will command the most dominating position of world importance. It will form a part of the trunk line of the Eurasian system which will connect the two populous centers, Europe and China, together. It will be the shortest line from the Pacific Coast to Europe. Its branch from Ili will connect with the future Indo-European line, and through Bagdad, Damascus and Cairo, will link up also with the future African system. Then there will be a through route from our projected port to Capetown. There is no existing railway commanding such a world important position as this.

Regarded from the principle of the "most urgent need

圖一
MAP 1

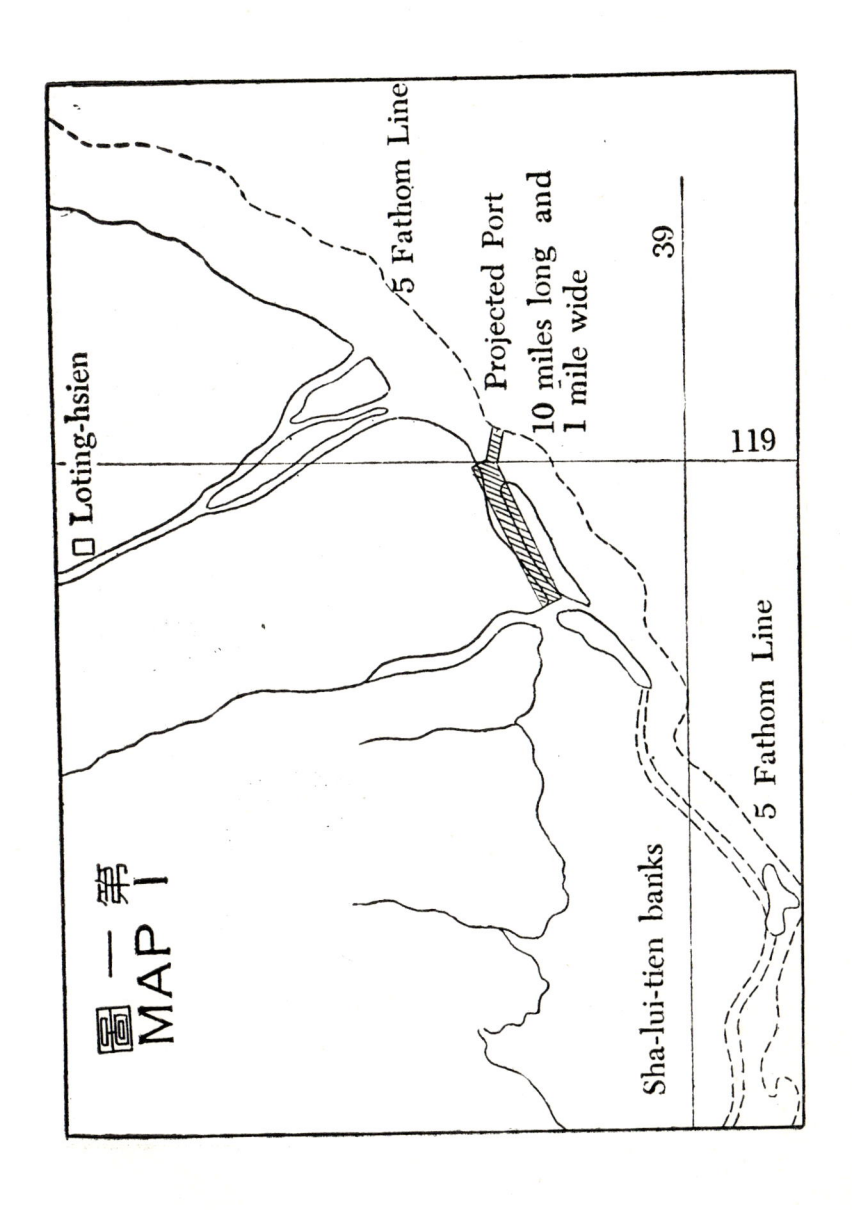

Loting-hsien

5 Fathom Line

Projected Port
10 miles long and
1 mile wide

39

119

Sha-lui-tien banks

5 Fathom Line

MAP II

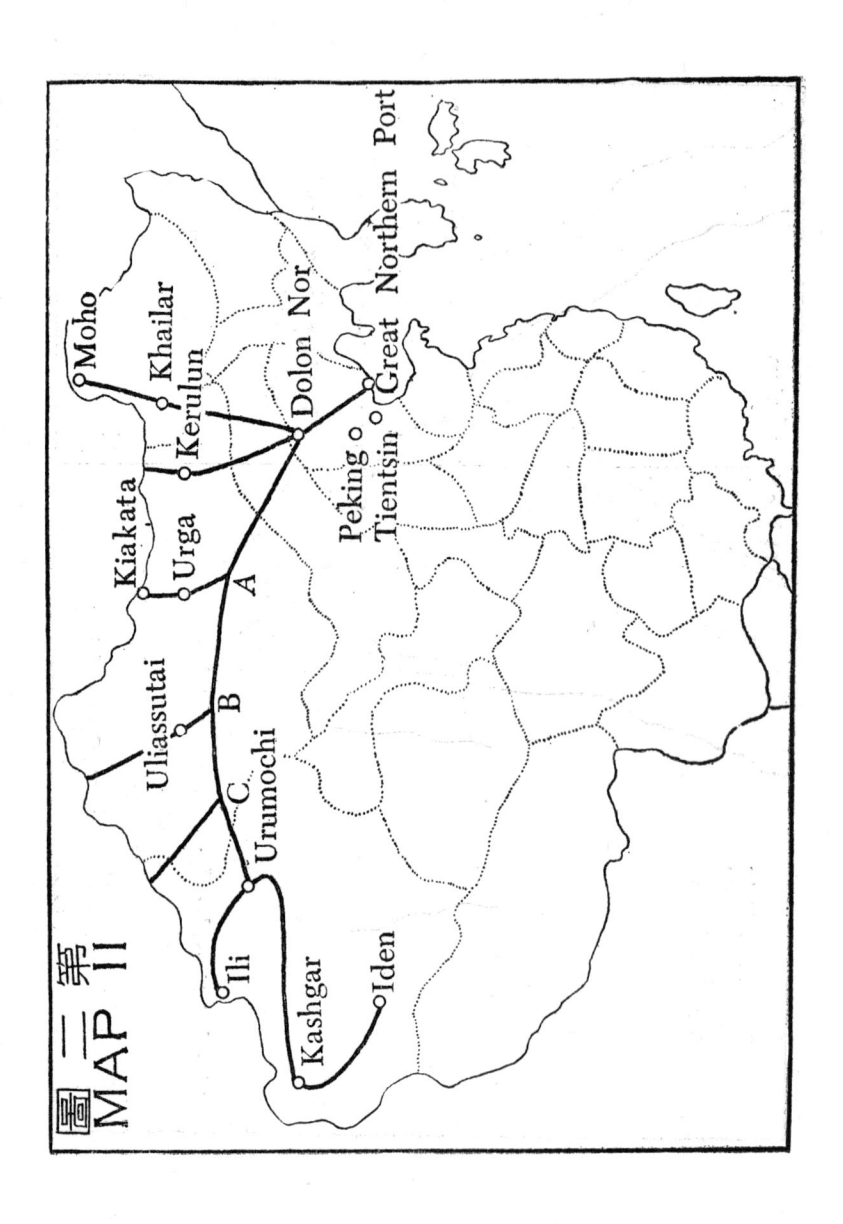

of the Nation," this railway system becomes the first in importance, for the territories traversed by it are larger than the eighteen provinces of China Proper. Owing to the lack of means of transportation and communication at present these rich territories are left undeveloped and millions of laborers in the congested provinces along the coast and in the Yangtze Valley are without work. What a great waste of natural and human energies. If there is a railway connecting these vast territories, the waste labor of the congested provinces can go and develop these rich soils for the good not only of China but also of the whole commercial world. So a system of railways to the northwestern part of the country is the most urgent need both politically and economically for China to-day.

I have intentionally left out the first principle—"the most remunerative field must be selected"—not because I want to neglect it but because I mean to call more attention to it and treat it more fully. It is commonly known to financiers and railway men that a railway in a densely populated country from end to end is the best paying proposition, and a railway in a thinly settled country from end to end is the least paying one. And a railway in an almost unpopulated country like our projected lines will take a long time to make it a paying business. That is why the United States Government had to grant large tracts of public lands to railway corporations to induce them to build the transcontinental lines to the Pacific coast, half a century ago. Whenever I talked with foreign railway men and financiers about the construction of railways to Mongolia and Sinkiang, they generally got very shy of the proposition. Undoubtedly they thought that it is for political and military reasons only that such a line as the Siberian Railway was built, which traversed through a thinly populated land. But they could not grasp the fact which might be entirely new to them, that a railway between a densely populated country and a sparsely settled country will pay far better than one that runs from end to end in a densely populated land. The reason is that in economic conditions the two ends of a well populated country are not so different as that between a thickly populated country and a newly opened country. At the two ends of a well populated country, in many respects, the local people are self-supplying, excepting a few special articles which they depend upon the other end of the road to supply. So the demand and supply between the two places are not very great, thus the trade between the two ends of the railway could not be very lucrative. While the difference of the economic condition between a well populated country and an unpopulated country is very great. The workers of the new land have to depend upon the supplies of the thickly populated country almost in everything excepting foodstuffs and raw materials which they have in abundance and for disposal of which they have to depend upon the demand of the well populated district. Thus the trade between the two ends of the line will be extraordinarily great. Furthermore, a railway in a thickly populated place will not affect much the masses which consist of the majority of the population. It is only the few well-to-do and the merchants and tradesmen that make use of it. While with a railway between a thickly populated country and a sparsely settled or unsettled country, as soon as it is opened to traffic for each mile, the masses of the congested country will use it and rush into the new land in a wholesale manner.

Thus the railway will be employed to its utmost capacity in passenger traffic from the beginning. The comparison between the Peking-Hankow Railway and the Peking-Mukden Railway in China is a convincing proof.

The Peking-Hankow Railway is a line of over eight hundred miles running from the capital of the country to the commercial center in the heart of China right along in an extraordinarily densely settled country from end to end. While the Peking-Mukden line is barely six hundred miles in length running from a thickly populated country to thinly populated Manchuria. The former is a well paying line put the later pays far better. The net profit of the shorter Peking-Mukden Line is sometimes three to four millions more yearly than that of the longer Peking-Hankow line.

Therefore, it is logically clear that a railway in a thickly populated country is much better than one that is in a thinly populated country in remuneration. But a railway between a very thickly populated and a very thinly populated or unpopulated country is the best paying proposition. This is a law in Railway Economics which hitherto had not been discovered by railway men and financiers.

According to this new railway economid law, our projected railway will be the best remunerative project of its kind. For at the one end, we have our projected port which acts as a connecting link with the thickly populated coast of China and the Yangtze Valley and also the two existing lines, the Kingham and the Tsinpu, as feeders to the projected port and the Dolon Nor line. And at the other end, we have a vast and rich territory, larger than China Proper, to be developed. There is no such vast fertile field so near to a center of a population of four hundred millions to be found in any other part of the world.

PART III

THE COLONIZATION OF MONGOLIA AND SINKIANG

The Colonization of Mongolia and Sinkiang is a complement of the Railway scheme. Each is dependent upon the other for its prosperity. The colonization scheme, besides benefitting the railway, is in itself a greatly profitable undertaking. The results of the United States, Canada, Australia, and Argentina are ample proofs of this. In the case of our project, it is simply a matter of applying waste Chinese labor and foreign machinery to a fertile land for production for which its remuneration is sure. The present Colonization of Manchuria, notwithstanding its topsy turvy way which caused great waste of land and human energy, has been wonderfully prosperous. If we would adopt scientific methods in our colonization project we could certainly obtain better results than all the others. Therefore, I propose that the whole movement be directed in a systematic way by state organization with the help of foreign experts and war organizers, for the good of the colonists particularly and the nation generally.

The land should be bought up by the state in order to prevent the speculators from creating the dog-in-the-manger system, to the detriment of the public. The land should be prepared and divided into farmsteads, then leased to colonists on perpetual term. The initial capital, seeds, implements and houses should be furnished by the state at cost price on cash or on the instalment plan. For these services, big organizations should be formed and war work measures should be adopted in order to transport, to feed, to clothe and to house every colonist on credit in his first year.

As soon as a sufficient number of colonists is settled in a district, franchise should be given for self-government and the colonists should be trained to manage their own local affairs with perfect democratic spirit.

If within ten years we can transport, let us say, ten millions of the people, from the congested provinces of China, to the Northwestern territory to develop its natural resources, the benefit to the commercial world at large will be enormous. No matter how big a capital that shall have been invested in the project it could be repaid within a very short time. So in regard to its bearing to "the principle of remuneration" there is no question about it.

Regarded from "the principle of the need of the Nation" colonization is the most urgent need of the first magnitude. At present China has more than a million soldiers to be disbanded. Besides, the dense population will need elbow room to move in. This Colonization project is the best thing for both purposes. The soldiers have to be disbanded at great expense and hundreds of millions of dollars may be needed for disbandment alone, in paying them off with a few months' pay. If nothing more could be done for these soldiers' welfare, they will either be left to starve or to rob for a living. Then the consequences will be unimaginable. This calamity must be prevented and prevented effectively. The best way for this is the colonization scheme. I hope that the friendly foreign financiers, who have the welfare of China at heart, when requested to float a reorganization loan for the Chinese Government in the future, will persist on the point—that the money furnished must first be used to carry out the colonization scheme for the disbanded soldiers. Otherwise, their money will only work disasters to China.

For the million or more of the soldiers to be disbanded, the district between our projected port and Dolon Nor is quite enough to accommodate them. This district is quite rich in mineral resources and is very sparsely settled. If a railway is to start at once from the projected port to Dolon Nor these soldiers could be utilized as a pioneer party for the work of the port, of the railway, of the developing of the adjacent land beyond the Great Wall, and of preparing Dolon Nor as a jumping ground for further colonization development of the great northern plain.

PART IV

The Construction of Canals to Connect the Inland Waterway Systems of North and Central China with the Great Northern Port

This scheme will include the regulation of the Hoangho and its branches, the Weiho in Shensi, and the Fenho in Shansi and connecting canals. The Hoangho should be deepened at its mouth in order to give a good drawing to clear its bed of silt and carry the same to the sea. For this purpose, jetties should be built far out to the deep sea, as those at the mouths of the Mississippi in America. Its embankments should be parallel in order to make the width of the channel equal right along, so as to give equal velocity to the current which will prevent the deposit of silt at the bottom. By dams and locks, it could be made navigable right up to Lanchow, in the province of Kansu, and at the same time water power could be developed. The Weiho and the Fenho can also be treated in the same manner so as to make them navigable to a great extent in the provinces of Shensi and Shansi. Thus the provinces of Kansu, Shensi, and Shansi can be connected by waterway with our projected port on the Gulf of Pechili, so that cheap carriage can be provided for the rich mineral and other products from these three hitherto secluded provinces.

The expenses of regulating the Hoangho may be very great. As a paying project, it may not be very attractive but as a flood preventive measure, it is the most important task to the whole nation. This river has been known as "China's Sorrow" for thousands of years. By its occasional overflow and bursting of its embankments, millions of lives and billions of money have been destroyed. It is a constant source of anxiety in the minds of all China's statesmen from time immemorial. A permanent safeguard must be effected, once for all, despite the expenses that will be incurred. The whole nation must bear the burden of its expenses. To deepen its mouth, to regulate its embankments and to build extra dykes are only half of the work to prevent flood. The entire reforestation of its watershed to prevent the washing off of loess is another half of the work in the prevention of flood.

The Grand Canal, the former Great Waterway of China between the North and the South for centuries, and now being reconstructed in certain sections, should be wholly reconstructed from end to end, in order to restore the inland waterway traffic from the Yangtze Valley to the North. The reconstruction of this canal will be a great remunerative concern for it runs right along from Tientsin to Hangchow in an extremely rich and populous country.

Another new canal should be constructed from our projected port to Tientsin to link up all the inland waterway systems to the new port. This new canal should be built extra wide and deep, let us say, similar to the present size of the Peiho, for the use of the coasting and shallow-draft vessels which the Peiho now accommodates for other than the winter seasons. The banks of this canal should be prepared for factory sites so as to enable it to pay not only by its traffic but also from the land on both sides of its banks.

As for planning and estimating these river and canal works, the assistance of technical experts must be solicited.

PART V

THE DEVELOPMENT OF THE IRON AND COAL FIELDS IN CHILI AND SHANSI, AND THE CONSTRUCTION OF IRON AND STEEL WORKS

Since we have in hand in this program the work of the construction of the Great Northern Port, the work of the building of a system of railways from the Great Northern

Port to the North Western Extremity of China, the work of the Colonization of Mongolia and Sinkiang, and the work of the construction of canals and improvement of rivers to connect with the Great Northern Port, the demand for materials will be very great. As the iron and coal resources of every industrial country are decreasing rapidly every year, and as all of them are contemplating the conservation of their natural resources for the use of future generations, if all the materials for the great development of China were to be drawn from them, the draining of the natural resources of those countries will be detrimental for their future generations. Besides, the present need of the post-bellum reconstruction of Europe has already absorbed all the iron and coal that the industrial world could supply. Therefore, new resources must be opened up to meet the extraordinary demand of the development of China.

The unlimited iron and coal fields of Shansi and Chili should be developed on a large scale. Let us say a capital of from five hundred to a thousand million dollars Mex. should be invested in this project. For as soon as the general development of China is started we would have created a vast market for iron and steel which the present industrial world will be unable to supply. Think of our railway construction, city building, harbor works, and various kinds of machineries and implements that will be needed! In fact, the development of China means the creation of a new need of various kinds of goods, for which, we must undertake to create the supply also, by utilizing the raw materials near by. Thus a great iron and steel works is an urgent necessity as well as a greatly profitable project.

In this First Program, we have followed the four principles set forth at the outset pretty closely. As needs create new needs and profits promote more profits, so our first program will be the forerunner of the other great developments, which we will deal with shortly.

PROGRAM II

As the Great Northern Port is the center of our first program, so the Great Eastern Port will be the center of our second program. I shall formulate this program as follows:

I. The Great Eastern Port.

II. The Regulating of the Yangtze Channel and Embankments.

III. The Construction of River Ports.

IV. The Improvement of Existing Waterways and Canals in Connection with the Yangtze.

V. The Establishment of Large Cement Works.

PART I

THE GREAT EASTERN PORT

Although Shanghai is already the largest port in all China, as it stands, it will not meet the future needs and demands of a world harbor. Therefore there is a movement at present among the foreign merchants in China to construct a world port in Shanghai. Several plans have been proposed such as to improve the existing arrangement, to build a wet dock by closing the Whangpoo, to construct a closed harbor on the right bank of the Yangtze outside of Whangpoo, and to excavate a new basin just east of Shanghai with a shipping canal to Hangchow Bay. It is estimated that a cost of over one hundred million dollars Mex. must be spent before Shanghai can be made a first-class port.

According to the four principles I set forth in Program I, Shanghai as a world port for Eastern China is not in an ideal position. The best position for a port of that kind is at a point just south of Chapu on the Hangchow Bay. This locality is far superior to Shanghai as an eastern port for China from the standpoint of our four principles as set forth in our first program. Henceforth, in our course of discussion, we shall call this the "Projected Port" so as to distinguish it from Shanghai, the existing port of Eastern China.

THE PROJECTED PORT

The "Projected Port" will be on the Bay which lies between the Chapu and the Kanpu promontories, a distance of about fifteen miles. A new sea wall should be built from one promontory to the other and a gap should be left at the Chapu end, a few hundred feet from the hill as an entrance to the harbor. The sea wall should be divided into five sections of three miles each. For the present, one section of three miles in length and one and a half miles in width should be built and a harbor of three or more square miles so formed would be sufficient. With the growth of commerce one section after another could be added to meet the needs. The front sea wall should be built of stone or concrete, while the transverse wall between the sea wall and the land side should be built of sand and bush mattress as a temporary structure to be removed in case of the extension of the harbor. Once a harbor is formed there need be no trouble regarding the future conservancy work, for there is no silt-carrying water in the vicinity by which the harbor and its approaches may be silted up afterwards. The entrance of our harbor is in the deepest part of the Hangchow Bay, and from the entrance to the open sea there is an average depth of six to seven fathoms at low water. The largest ocean liner could therefore come into port at any hour. Thus as a first-class seaport in Central China our Projected Port is superior to Shanghai. See Map III.

From the viewpoint of the principle of the line of least resistance, our Projected Port will be on new land which will offer absolute freedom for city planning and industrial development. All public utilities and transportation plants can be constructed according to the most up-to-date methods. This point alone is an important factor for a future city like ours which in time is bound to grow as large as New York City. If one hundred years ago human foresight could have foreseen the present size and population of New York, much of the labor and money spent could have been saved and blunders due to shortsightedness avoided in meeting conditions of the ever growing population and commerce of that city. With this in view a great Eastern Port in China should be started on new ground to insure room for growth proportionate to its needs.

Moreover, all the natural advantages which Shanghai possesses as a central mart and Yangtze Port in Eastern China are also possessed by our Projected Port. Furthermore, our Projected Port in comparison with Shanghai is of shorter distance, by rail communication, to all the large cities south of the Yangtze. And if the existing waterway between this part of the country and Wuhu were improved then the water communication with the upper Yangtze would also be shorter from our Projected Port than from Shanghai. And all the artificial advantages possessed by Shanghai as a large city and a commercial center in this part of China can be easily attained by our Projected Port within a short time.

Comparing Shanghai with our Projected Port from a remunerative point of view in our development scheme, the former is much inferior in position to the latter, for valuable lands have to be bought and costly plants and existing arrangements have to be scrapped the cost of which alone is enough to construct a fine harbor on our projected site. Therefore, it is highly advisable to construct another first-class port for Eastern China like the one I here propose, leaving Shanghai to be an inland mart and manufacturing center as Manchester is in relation to Liverpool, Osaka to Kobe, and Tokyo to Yokohama.

Our Projected Port will be a highly remunerative proposition for the cost of construction will be many times cheaper than Shanghai and the work simpler. The land between Chapu and Kanpu and farther on will not cost more than fifty to one hundred dollars a mow. The State should take up a few hundred square miles of land in this neigborhood for the scheme of our future city development. Let us say two hundred square miles of land at the price of one hundred dollars a mow be taken up. As six mows make an acre and six hundred and forty acres a square mile, two hundred square miles would cost 76,000,000 dollars Mex. An enormous sum for a project indeed! But the land could be fixed at the present price and the State could buy only that part of land which will immediately be taken up and used. The other part of the land would remain as State land unpaid for and left to the original owners' use without the right to sell. Thus the State only takes up as

第三圖 MAP III

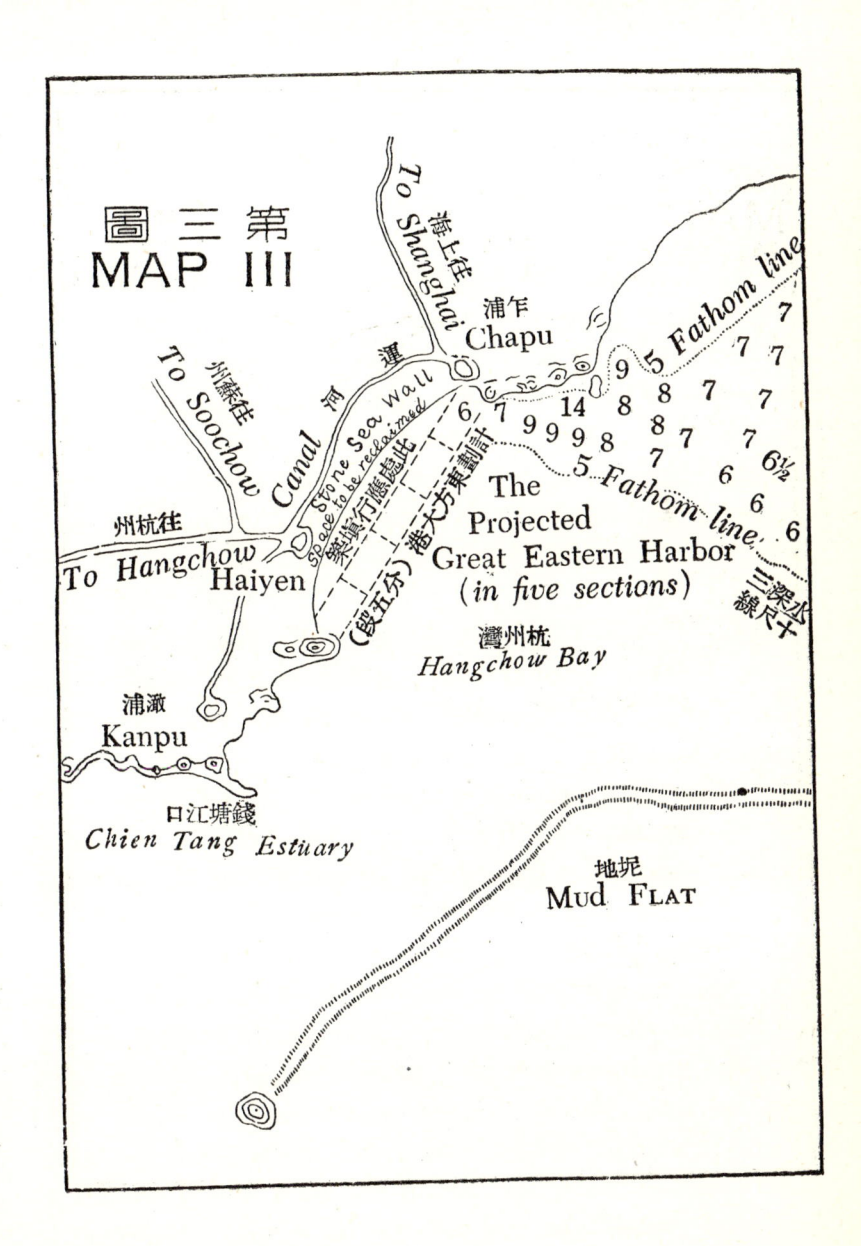

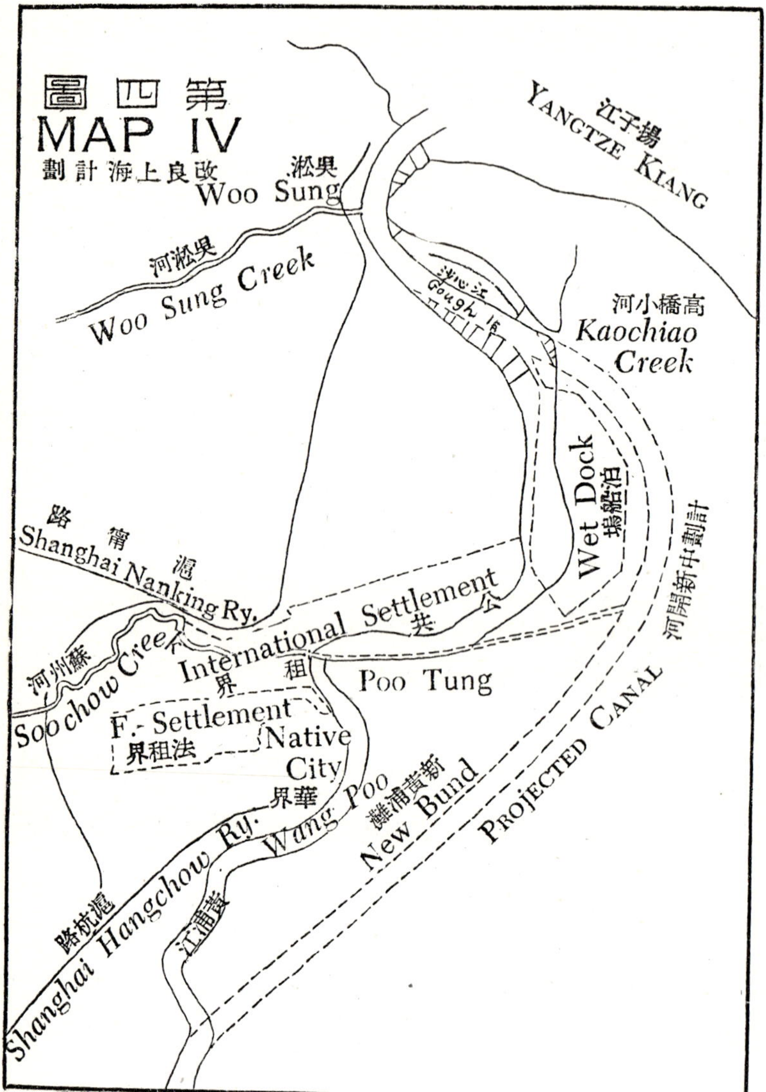

第四圖
MAP IV
改良上海計劃
吳淞
Woo Sung
吳淞河
Woo Sung Creek
揚子江
YANGTZE KIANG
江心沙
Gough Is.
高橋小河
Kaochiao Creek
泊船場
Wet Dock
計劃中新開河
PROJECTED CANAL
滬甯路
Shanghai Nanking Ry.
蘇州河
Soochow Creek
公共租界
International Settlement
Poo Tung
法租界
F.-Settlement
Native City
華界
新黃浦灘
New Bund
Wang Poo
黃浦江
滬杭路
Shanghai Hangchow Ry.

much land as it could use in the development scheme at a fixed price which remains permanent. The payment then would be gradual. The State could pay for the land from its unearned increment afterwards. So that only the first allotment of land has to be paid for from the capital fund; the rest will be paid for by its own future value. After the first section of the harbor is completed and the port developed, the price of land then would be bound to rise rapidly, and within ten years the land value within the city limits would rise to various grades from a thousand to a hundred thousand dollars per mow. Thus the land itself would be a source of profit. Besides there would also be the profit from the scheme itself, i.e., the harbor and the city. Because of its commanding position, the harbor has every possibility of becoming a city equal to New York. It would probably be the only deep-water seaport for the Yangtze Valley and beyond, an area peopled by two hundred million inhabitants, twice the population of the whole States. The rate of growth of such a city would be in proportion to the rate of progress of the working out of the development scheme. If war work methods, that is, gigantic planning and efficient organization, were applied to the construction of the harbor and city, then an Oriental New York City would spring up in a very short time.

SHANGHAI AS THE GREAT EASTERN PORT

If only to provide a deep-water harbor for the future commerce in this part of China is our object then there is no question about the choice between Shanghai and our Projected Port. From every point of view Shanghai is doomed. However, in our scheme of development of China,

Shanghai has certain claims for our consideration which may prove its salvation as an important city. The curse of Shanghai as a world port for future commerce is the silt of the Yangtze which fills up all its approaches rapidly every year. This silt, according to the estimation of Mr. Von Heidenstam, Engineer-in-chief of the Whangpoo Conservancy Board, is a hundred million tons a year and is sufficient to cover an area of forty square miles ten feet deep. So before Shanghai can be considered ever likely to become a world port this silt problem must first be solved. Fortunately, in our program, we have the regulation of the Yangtze Channels and Embankments, which will cooperate in solving the problem of Shanghai. Thus with this scheme in mind we might just as well consider that the silt question of Shanghai has been solved and let us go ahead, while leaving the regulation of the Yangtze Estuary to the next part, to deal with the improvement of the Shanghai Harbor.

There are many plans proposed by experts for improving the Shanghai Harbor as stated before and some of them will necessitate the scrapping of all the work which has been done by the Whangpoo Conservancy Board for the last twelve years, at the cost of eleven million taels. Here I wish to present a layman's plan for the consideration of specialists and the public.

My project for the construction of a world harbor in Shanghai is to leave the existing arrangement intact from the mouth of the Whangpoo to the junction of Kao Chiao Creek above Gough Island. Thus all the work hitherto done by the Whangpoo Conservancy Board for the last twelve years will be saved. The plan is to cut a new canal from the junction of Kao Chiao Creek right into Pootung to prolong that part of the channel which has been completed by the Conservancy Work, and to enlarge the curve along the right side of the Whangpoo River and join it again, at the second turn above Lunghwa Railway Junction, so as to make the river from that point to a point opposite Yangtzepoo Point almost in a straight line and hence a gentle curve to Woosung. This new canal would encircle nearly thirty square miles of land which would form the civic center and the New Bund of our future Shanghai. Of course the present crooked Whangpoo right in front of Shanghai would have to be filled up to form boulevards and business lots. It goes without saying that the reclaimed lots from the Whangpoo would become State property and the land between this and the new river and beyond should be taken up by the State and put at the disposal of the International Development Organization. Thus it may be possible for Shanghai to compete with our Projected Port economically in its construction and therefore to attract foreign capital, to the improvement of Shanghai as a future world port. See Map IV.

Below Yangtzepoo Point I propose to build a wet dock. This dock should be laid between the left bank of the present Whangpoo, from Yangtzepoo Point to the turn above Gough Island and the left bank of the new river. The space of the dock should be about six square miles. A lock entrance is to be constructed at the point above Gough Island. The wet dock should be forty feet deep and the new river can also be made the same depth by flushing with the water, not as proposed by experts, from a lock canal between the Yangtze and the Taihu, at Kiangyin, but from our improved waterway between this part of the country and Wuhu so that a much stronger current could be obtained.

As we see that the present Whangpoo has to be reclaimed from the second turn above Lunghwa Railway Junction to Yangtzepoo Point for city planning, then the question of how to dispose of the Soochow Creek must be answered. I propose that this stream should be led alongside the right bank of the future defunct river and straight on to the upper end of the wet dock, thence joining the new canal. At the point of contact of the Creek and the wet dock a lock entrance may be provided in order to facilitate water traffic from Soochow as well as the inland water system directly with the wet dock.

As the first principle in our program was remuneration, all our plans must strictly follow this principle. To create Pootung Point, therefore, as a civic center and to build a new Bund farther on along the left bank of the new canal in order to increase the value of the new land which would result from this scheme must be kept in mind. Only by so doing would the construction of Shanghai as a deep harbor be worth while. And only by creating some new and valuable property in this fore-doomed port could Shanghai be saved from the competition of our Projected Port. After all, the most important factor for the salvation of Shanghai is the solution of the Yangtze Estuaries. Now let us see what effect and bearing the regulating of the Yangtze Channel and Embankments have upon the question, and this we are going to deal with in the next part.

PART II

The Regulating of the Yangtze River

The regulating of the Yangtze River may be divided as follows:

a. From the deep-water line of the sea to Whangpoo Junction.

b. From Whangpoo Junction to Kiangyin.

c. From Kiangyin to Wuhu.

d. From Wuhu to Tungliu.

e. From Tungliu to Wusueh.

f. From Wusueh to Hankow.

A. Regulating of the Estuary from Deep-Water Line up to the Junction of Whangpoo

It is a natural law that the obstruction to navigation in all rivers is begun at their mouths, therefore the improvement of any river for navigation must start from the estuary. The Yangtze River is no exception to this rule, therefore to regulate the Yangtze, we must begin by dealing with its estuaries.

The Yangtze has three estuaries, namely: The North Branch lying between the left bank and the Island of Tsungming, the North Channel lying between the Tsungming Island and the Tungsha Banks and the South Channel lying between the Tungsha Banks and the right bank. Henceforth for the sake of convenience I shall call them the North, Middle, and South Channels.

The silting up of a river's mouth is due to the loss of velocity in its current when the water gets into the wide opening at its junction with the sea and causes the silt to deposit there. The remedy is to maintain the velocity of the current by narrowing the mouth of the river so that it equals that of the upper part. In this way the silt is suspended in the water moving on into the deep sea. The narrowing process may be accomplished by walls or training jetties. And thus the silt may be carried by the water into the deepest part of the open sea and before it settles down upon the bottom a returning tide will carry it from the approach into the shallow parts on both sides of the river's mouth. The mouth of a river can be kept clear from deposit of silt by the action and reaction of the ebb and flow tide. The conservancy of an estuary of any river is accomplished by utilizing these natural forces.

In order to regulate the estuary of the Yangtze we have to study the three channels which form its mouth and to find out which of these channels is to be selected as the regulated entrance ino the sea. In Mr. Von Heidenstam's proposal for the improvement of the approach of Shanghai Harbor, he recommends two alternatives, viz., either to block up the North and Middle Channels and to leave the South Channel only for the mouth of the Yangtze, or to train the South Channel only and leave the other two alone. For the present, he thinks, perhaps for the sake of economy, the latter scheme would be enough. But the training of the South Channel alone as the approach to Shanghai would leave it in a state of perpetual anxiety as has been apprehended by Mr. Von Heidenstam and other experts, for the main volume of the water of the Yangtze may be diverted into either of the other two channels and leave the Southern one to be silted up at any time. Therefore to make the approach of Shanghai once for all safe and permanent, it is necessary to block up two of the three channels, leaving only one as an approach to the port. This is also the only feasible way of regulating the estuary of the Yangtze.

In our scheme of regulating the Yangtze Estuary I should recommend using the North Channel only and to block the other two. Because the North Channel is the shortest way to the deep-sea line and by using it as the only mouth of the Yangtze, we have on both sides of it more shallow banks to be reclaimed by its silt. Thus the expenditure would be less and the results greater. But this would leave Shanghai in the lurch. Therefore in a cooperative scheme like this I would apply the theory of killing two birds with one stone by using the Middle Channel, since it would suit both of our purposes. The reason for this is because the regulating of the Yangtze Estuary and the securing of a Shanghai approach have different purposes, hence we must consider them differently.

In my project of regulating the Yangtze Estuary I have two aims, namely, to secure a deep channel to the open sea and to save as much silt as possible for the purpose of reclamation of land. The Middle Channel provides three ready receptacles for the deposit of the silt for the formation of new land: the Haimen, the Tsungming, and the Tungsha Banks. Besides these banks there are many hundreds of square miles of shallow bottom which in the course of ten or twenty years will also form land. As remuneration is our first principle we must consider it in every step of our progress. The reclamation of about a thousand square miles of land even in forty not to say twenty years would be ample profit. At the lowest estimate the reclaimed land would be worth twenty dollars per mow. If after ten years five hundred square miles would be ready for cultivation purposes then we would gain a profit of 38,000,000 dollars. Whereas to make an approach by the South Channel the receptacle ground will be on one side only, that is, the Tungsha Banks, while on the right of the approach is the deep Hangchow Bay which would take hundreds of years to fill up, and in the meanwhile half of the silt would be wasted. To Shanghai as a seaport the silt is a curse but to the shallow banks the silt would be a blessing.

Since it is a profitable undertaking to reclaim the above mentioned banks and the neighboring shallows, we can quite well afford to build a double stone wall from the shore end of the Yangtze right out into the deep sea far beyond Shaweishan Island which is a distance of about forty miles. A stone wall from one fathom to five fathoms in height at low-water level would likely not exceed an average cost of two hundred thousand dollars a mile as cheap stone can easily be obtained from the granite islands nearby, in the Chusan Archipelago. A wall of forty miles on each side that is eighty miles in all will cost sixteen million dollars or thereabouts. And considering that 200 or 300 square miles of Haimen, Tsungming, and the Tungsha banks could be converted into arable land within a short time, the expense of building the wall is well justified. Furthermore, the construction of this wall means that there will be a safe and permanent approach for a world port in Shanghai as well as a deep outlet for the Yangtse. See Map V.

The regulating wall on the right side should be built from the junction of the Whangpoo by prolongation of its right jetty describing a gentle curve into the depths of the South Channel and turning toward the opposite side and cutting through the Blockhouse Island into the Middle Channel, then running eastward right into the five-fathom line southeast of Shaweishan Island. The left wall would be a continuation from that of Tsungming at Tsungpaosha Island parallel with the right wall by a distance of about two miles. This wall should curve to a point at or near Drinkwater Point at Tsungming Island, then project into the five-fathom line at the open sea passing by just at the south side of the Shaweishan Island. A glance at the map here attached would be sufficient to show how the future outlet of the Yangtze as well as the future approach of Shanghai should be. The two regulating submerged walls on both sides would be as high as low-water level so as to give a free passage of the water over the top at flood tide. This will serve the purpose of carrying back the silt from the sea when the tide comes in, thus to reclaim the shallow spaces inclosed behind the walls on both sides of the river more quickly than otherwise. The new channel formed by these two parallel walls would likely be deeper than the present South Channel outside th Whangpoo, which is forty to fifty feet deep because the velocity of the current will be greater than the present one, due to the concentration of three channels into one. Furthermore, the depth would be more uniform and stable than at present. Although the regulating walls end at the five-fathom line, the momentum of the current would continue beyond that point, and so would cut into the deep water outside. This would serve the double purpose of draining the Yangtze Estuary as well as keeping open the approach to Shanghai.

B. FROM WHANGPOO JUNCTION TO KIANGYIN

This part of the channel of the Yangtze River is most irregular and changeable. The widest part is over ten miles while the Kiangyin Narrow is only but three-quarters of a mile. The depth of the channel at the open part is from five to ten fathoms while that of Kiangyin Narrow is twenty fathoms. Judging by the depth of the water at this point a width of one and a half miles must be provided for the channel in order to slow down the current and to give a uniform velocity right along the river. So the two-mile wide channel at Whangpoo Junction has to be tabulated into one mile and a half at Kiangyin. See Map VI.

The north or left embankment commencing at Tsungpao Sha continues with the sea wall and makes a convex curve up to Tsungming Island at a point about six miles northwest from Tsungming city. Then it follows along the shore of Tsungming right up to Mason Point and transversing across the north channel parallel to the north shore at a distance of three or four miles right up to Kinshan Point, thence it cuts across the deep channel which was formed in recent years and curves southwestward to join the shore northeast of Tsingkiang and follows the shore line for a distance of about seven or eight miles, then cuts into the land side to give this part of the river a width of one and

第五圖
MAP V

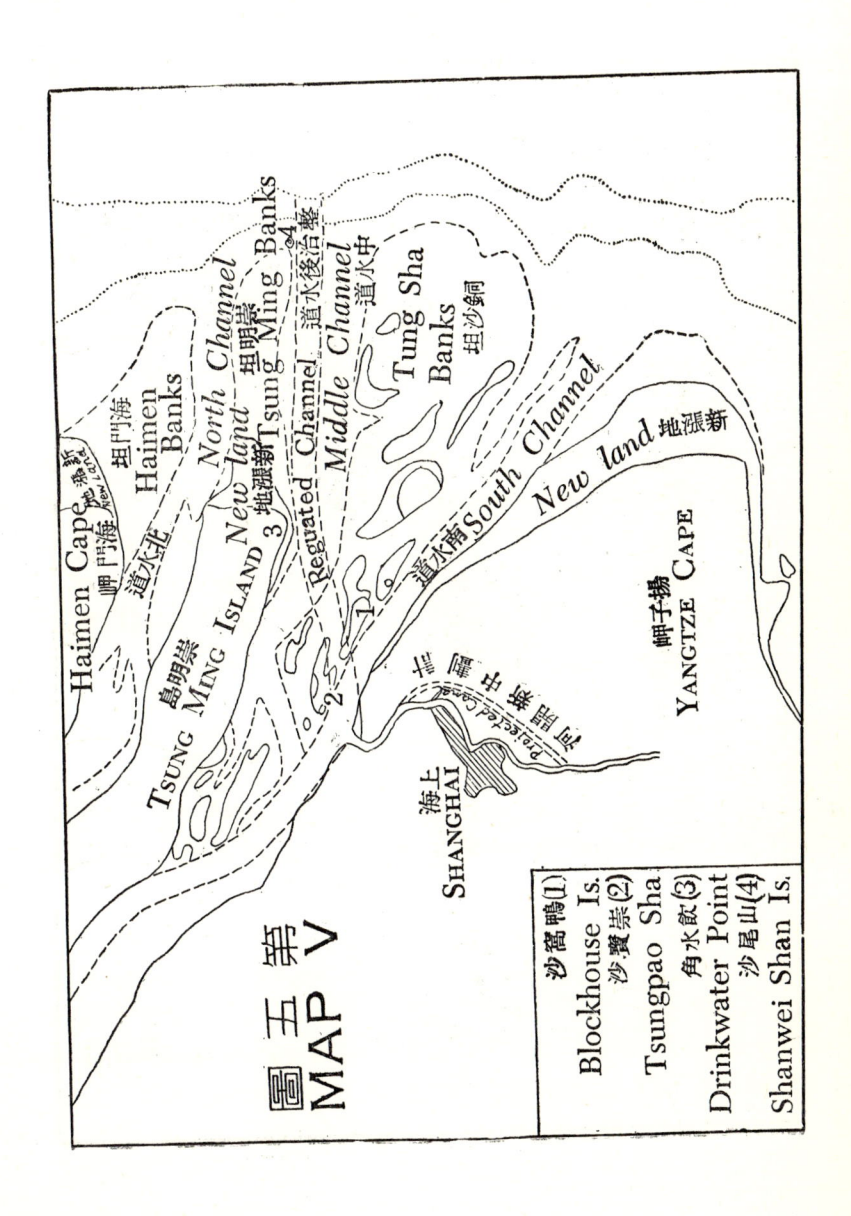

Blockhouse Is. 沙鴉鴨(1)
Tsungpao Sha 沙寶崇(2)
Drinkwater Point 角水飲(3)
Shanwei Shan Is. 沙毛山(4)

Haimen Cape 岬漁新
Haimen Banks 崇門海 道水北
North Channel
New land 地塹新
Tsung Ming Island 島明崇
Tsung Ming Banks 崇明坦 道水後治
Regulated Channel 道水理
Middle Channel
Tung Sha Banks 銅沙坦 道水中
South Channel 道水甫
New land 地漲新
Yangtze Cape 岬子揚
Shanghai 海上
Projected 堤中垸盟

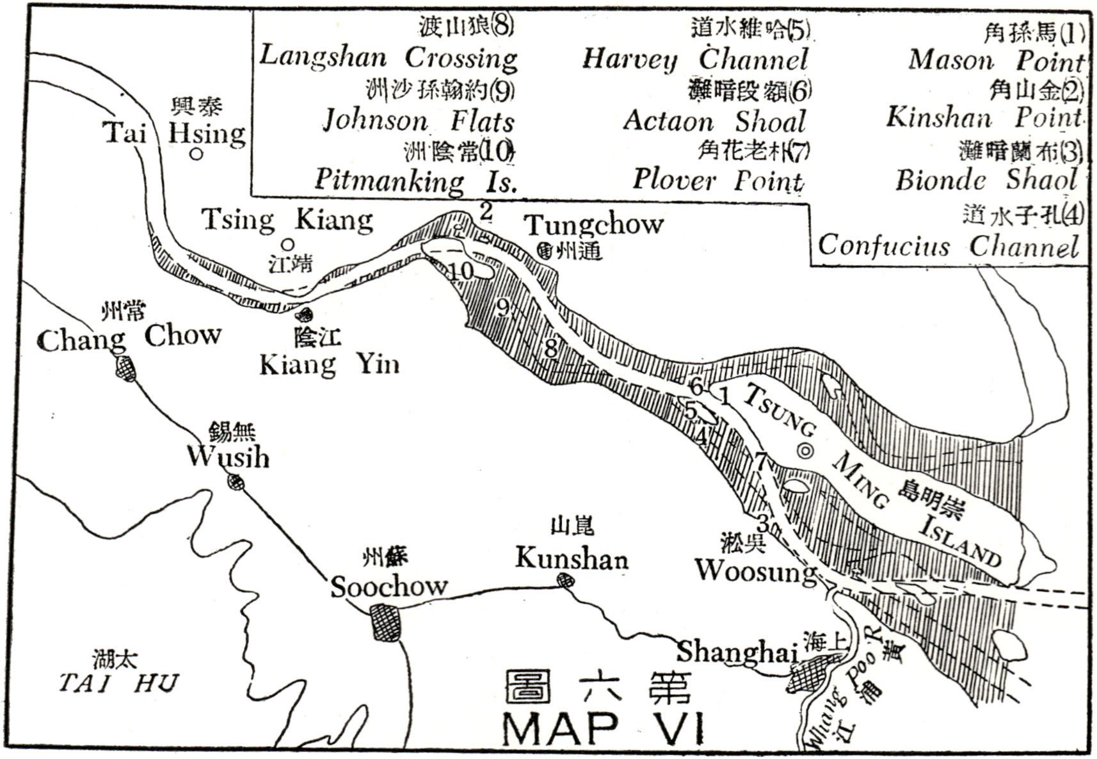
渡山狼(8)
Langshan Crossing
洲沙孫翰約(9)
Johnson Flats
洲陰常(10)
Pitmanking Is.
道水維哈(5)
Harvey Channel
灘暗段額(6)
Actaon Shoal
角花老朴(7)
Plover Point
角孫馬(1)
Mason Point
角山金(2)
Kinshan Point
灘暗蘭布(3)
Bionde Shoal
道水子孔(4)
Confucius Channel
興泰
Tai Hsing
Tsing Kiang
江靖
Tungchow
州通
州常
Chang Chow
陰江
Kiang Yin
錫無
Wusih
州蘇
Soochow
山崑
Kunshan
淞吳
Woosung
Tsung Ming Island
島明崇
海上
Shanghai
Whang Poo R.
江浦黃
湖太
TAI HU
圖六第
MAP VI

a half miles from the fort at the Kiangyin side. This embankment from Tsungpao Sha to Tsingkiang Point opposite Kiangyin fort is about one hundred miles in length.

South of Tsungming Island a part of this embankment and a part of the wall that projects into the sea together inclose a shallow space of about 160 square miles good for reclamation purposes. The other part of the embankment, which runs from Mason Point at the head of Tsungming Island to Tsingkiang shore, incloses another space of about 130 square miles.

The right embankment starts at the end of the left jetty of Whangpoo Junction and, skirting along the Paoshan shore and passing the Blonde Shoal into the deep, crosses the Confucius Channel on into Actaon Shoal and follows the right side of Harvey Channel on to Plover Point. Then it turns northwest across the deep channel into Langshan Flats, thence recrosses the deep channel at Langshan crossing into Johnson Flats, then joins the Pitman King Island, and thence skirts along the shore right into the foot of the hills at Kiangyin forts. This embankment incloses two shallow spaces: one above and the other below Plover Point, together about 160 square miles. Alongside of both of these embankments there are shallow spaces amounting to about 450 square miles, a great part of which having already formed land and a part already appearing in low water. When these spaces are cut off from the moving current the process of reclamation would be made to work more rapidly so it is not extravagant to hope that within the course of twenty years the whole of these 450 square miles would be completely reclaimed and ready for cultivation. The profits from the new lands thus reclaimed would amount to about $29,760,000 if only taken at $20 per mow. The profits from the new lands would be netted from the beginning of the work and would increase every year up to the completion of the reclamation process.

With a profit of $30,000,000 in the course of twenty years before us, it is a worth-while proposition to take up. Now let us see what amount of capital should be invested before the whole project of our reclamation work could be completed. In order to reclaim this 450 square miles of land two hundred miles of embankments have to be built. Part of these projected embankments will be along the shore line, a greater part will be in midstream, and a small part in deep channel. Those along the shore line need not be bothered with except that the concave surface must be protected with stone or concrete work. Those in midstream should be filled up with stone ten feet or less below low-water level just enough to give a resistance to the undercurrent in order to prevent it from running sideward. Thus the main current would follow the line of least resistance and cut the channel, as directed by the rudimental embankment, by its own force. This rudimental embankment would cost less than the sea wall which I estimated at $200,000 per mile. Except at one point, that is, the junction of the North Channel at Mason Point, which has to be blocked up entirely, the cost for which, as has been estimated by experts, would amount to over a million dollars for a distance of two or three miles. Thus the profits accuring from the reclaimed lands would be quite sufficient to pay for the embankments. So far we see that the regulating of the Yangtze from the sea to Kiangyin is a selfpaying proposition from the reclamation of land alone, aside from the improvement of the navigation of the Yangtze River.

C. FROM KIANGYIN TO WUHU

This part of the river is quite different in nature from that below Kiangyin. Its channel is more stable and only in a few places sharp curves occur and the water has cut into the concave sides of the land, thus occasionally making new channels along the sides of the two shores. This section of the river is about 180 miles in length. See Map VII.

The regulating works here would be more complicated than those below Kiangyin. For besides the dilated parts which have to be reclaimed in the same manner as those of the lower part of the river, the sharp curves have to be straightened and side channels have to be blocked, and midstream islands have to be removed, and narrows have to be widened to give uniform width to the river. However, most of the existing embankments in this part could be left as they are except some of the concave surfaces of the shores have to be protected by either stone or concrete work. The regulating works of the channel and the embankments can be done by artificial means as well as by natural processes so as to economize as much as possible. The cost of the whole works of this part of the river cannot be accurately estimated until a detail survey is made; but in a rough guess $400,000 per mile may not be very far from the mark. Thus 180 miles will cost $72,000,000 exclusive of the expenses for the widening of the point between Nanking and Pukow, in which case valuable properties will have to be removed.

The Kwachow cut is to straighten the three sharp curves in front of and above Chinkiang by converting them into one. Two and a half miles of the land in the northern shore opposite Chinkiang will have to be cut into in order to form a new channel of a mile or more in width. The part of the river in front of, and above and below Chinkiang has to be reclaimed. The new land thus reclaimed would form the water front of Chinkiang city, the value of which may be sufficient to defray the cost of the work and compensate for the land taken away on the northern shore, to form the new channel. So the works of this part will be at least a self-paying proposition.

The narrow between Pukow and Hsiakwan from pier to pier is barely six cables wide. The depth of the water in this narrow from the shallowest to the deepest is six to twenty-two fathoms. The land of the Hsiakwan side had occasionally sunk away on account of the too rapid current and the depth of the water. This indicates that this part is too narrow for the volume of the Yangtze water to pass. Therefore a wider passage must be provided for. In order to do so, the whole town of Hsiakwan must be sacrificed as the river must be widened right up to the foot of the Lion Hill, so as to provide a passage of a mile wide at this point. What the cost for the compensation of this valuable property of Hsiakwan will be will have to be submitted to the experts for a careful investigation before it can be determined. This will be the most costly part of the whole project for the regulating of the Yangtze. But

第七圖 MAP VII

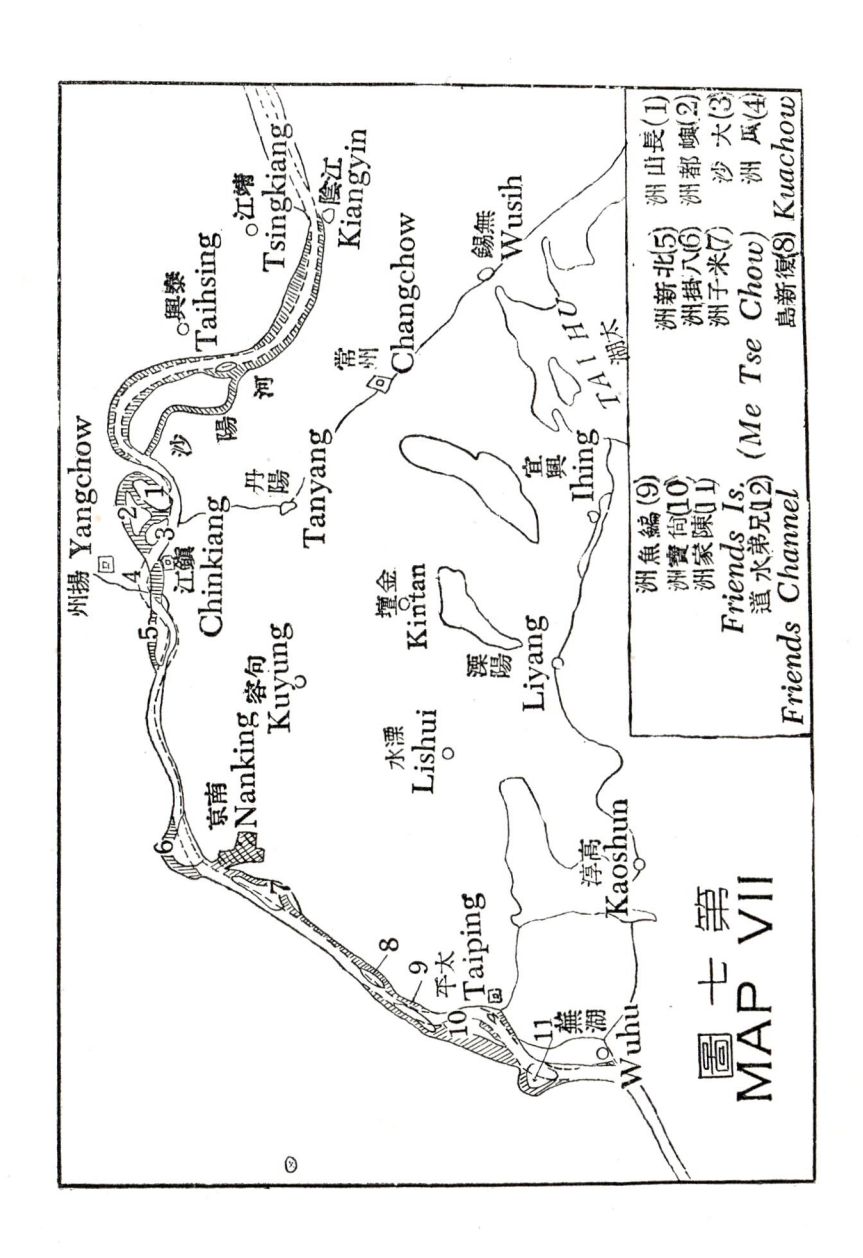

揚州 Yangchow
江鎮 Chinkiang
容句 Kuyung
南京 Nanking
太平 Taiping
蕪湖 Wuhu
高淳 Kaoshun
溧水 Lishui
金壇 Kintan
溧陽 Liyang
宜興 Ihing
丹陽 Tanyang
常州 Changchow
無錫 Wusih
江陰 Kiangyin
江嘴 Tsingkiang
泰興 Taihsing
沙河

太湖 TAI HU

(1) 長山洲
(2) 都都嶼洲
(3) 大沙洲
(4) 瓜洲 Kuachow
(5) 新北洲
(6) 八掛洲
(7) 米子洲
(8) 新復島
(9) 編魚洲
(10) 寶倘洲
(11) 陳家洲
(12) 水道兄弟 Friends Is. (Me Tse Chow)
Friends Channel

第八圖 MAP VIII

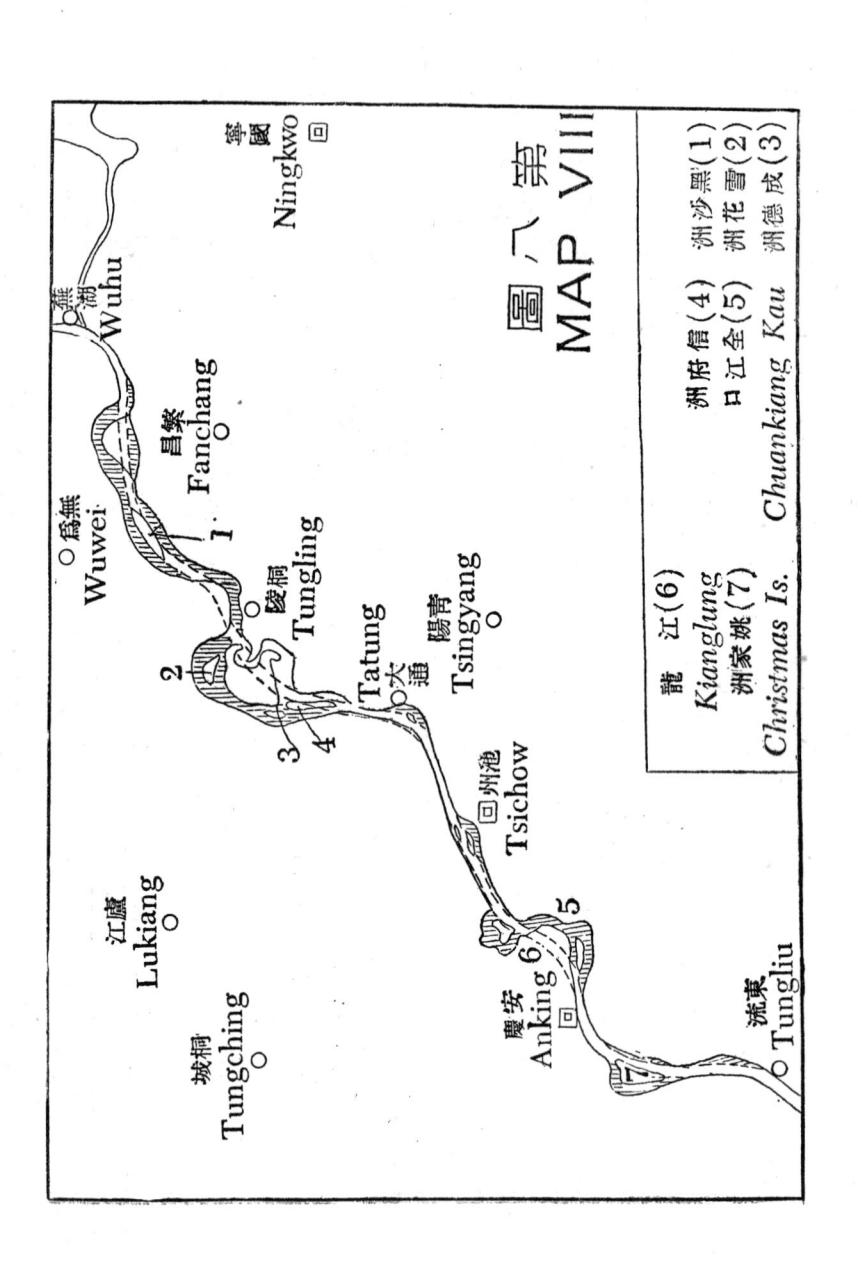

黑沙洲 (1) Chuankiang Kau
雪花洲 (2)
成德洲 (3)
信府洲 (4)
全江口 (5)
龍 江 (6) Kianglung
姚家洲 (7) Christmas Is.

Ningkwo 寧國
Wuhu 蕪湖
Fanchang 繁昌
Wuwei 無爲
Tungling 銅陵
Tatung 大通
Tsingyang 靑陽
Tsichow 池州
Lukiang 盧江
Tungching 桐城
Anking 安慶
Tungliu 東流

undoubtedly some equally valuable property can be created along the riverside near by in place of Hsiakwan, so that a balance may be realized by the work itself.

The channel below the Nanking Pukow Narrow will follow the short passage alongside of the foot of the Mofushan to Wulungshan. The loop around the island north of Nanking will have to be blocked up in order to straighten the course of the river.

The section of the river from Nanking to Wuhu is almost in a straight line with three dilatations along its course one just above Nanking the other two just above and below the East and West pillars. To regulate the first dilatation the channel above Me-tse-chow should be blocked up and the island outside of it should be partly cut to widen the proper channel. To regulate the other two dilatations the river should be made to curve toward Taiping Fu to follow the deep channel on the right bank. The left channel should be blocked up. The islands along this curve should be partly or wholly removed. To regulate the dilatation above the Pillars, the Friends Channel should be blocked up and Friends Island be partly cut away. And the left bank below Wuhu should also be cut to give the channel a uniform width.

D. FROM WUHU TO TUNGLIU

This part of the river is about 130 miles in length. Along its course there are six dilatations, the most prominent of which is the one that lies immediately below Tungling, which extends over ten miles from side to side. In each of these dilatations there are usually two or three channels with newly formed islands between them. The deep passage often changes from one side to the other, and it is not uncommon that all of the channels are filled up at the same time, thus stopping navigation altogether for a considerable period. See Map VIII.

In regulating the part of the river from ten miles above Wuhu to ten miles below Tatung, I propose to cut a new channel through the midstream islands formed by the three dilatations and the sharp corners of the shore, in order to straighten as well as to shorten the river, as marked by the dotted lines in the map attached here. The cost of the cut could not be estimated until a detail survey is made. But as soon as the embankments are laid out the natural force of the river's own current will do a great part of the dredging work, so that the expenses of the cutting for the new channel will be much less than usual. Above Tatung there are two sharp turns of the left shore to be cut. One is on the left shore at the point where the beacon now stands about twelve miles from Tatung. In this place a few miles of the left shore will have to be cut away. The other cut is just below the city of Anking hence to Kianglung beacon, a distance of about six miles. By this cut we do away with the sharp turns of the river at Chuan Kiang Kau. These cuttings would cost much more than the piling of stone at the lower reach of the river. It is quite certain that the reclamation of the side channels of this part will not cover the cost of the cuttings. Therefore this part of the regulating work will not be self-paying, but the navigation of the Yangtze, the protection it gives to both sides of the land, and the prevention of floods in the future will amply compensate for such work.

E. FROM TUNGLIU TO WUSUEH

This part of the river is about eighty miles in length. The land along the right bank is generally hilly while that along the left is low. Along its course there are four dilatations. In three of these dilatations the current has cut into the left or northern bank of the river and then turns back into its main course again almost at right angles. At such points the bank is very unstable. Between the channels of these dilatations islands are being formed. See Map IX.

The regulating works of this part are much easier to construct than those of the lower part. The three diverting semicircular channels have to be blocked up at the upper ends, and the lower openings left open for silt to go into at flood seasons in order to reclaim them by the natural process. The other dilatations should be narrowed in from both sides by jetties. A few places will have to be cut, the most important being the Pigeon Island and the turn above Siau Ku Shan. Some of the midstream islands will have to be removed, and a few wide places filled up in order to make the channel uniform, so as to give a regular minimum depth of six fathoms right along the whole course.

F. FROM WUSUEH TO HANKOW

This part of the river is about one hundred miles long. Above Wusueh we enter into the hilly country on both sides. The river here is generally about half a mile wide, with a depth of from five to twelve fathoms or sometimes more in certain places. See Map X.

To regulate this part of the river a few wide spaces have to be reclaimed to give a uniform channel, and the side channels at three or four places closed up. Then we can make a channel with a uniform depth of from six to eight fathoms at all seasons. At Collison Island section of the river the Ayres Channel has to be closed up, leaving the winter channel alone so as to give a gentle curve above and below this island. At Willes Island and Gravenor Island point the Round Channel and the channel between these two islands must be blocked up. The river must be made to cut through Willes Island to make a shorter curve. At Bouncer Island the South channel must be blocked up and above this the Low Point turn must be cut away to form a gentler curve. From this point to Hankow the river should be made narrower first by reclaiming the right side as far as the meeting of the southwest curve with the right bank then the reclamation should start at the opposite side of the left bank and right up along the front of Hankow Settlement until the Han River Mouth is reached. Thus a depth of six to eight fathoms can be secured right up to the Bund of Hankow.

To sum up, the whole length of the regulating course of the river from the deep sea to Hankow is about 630 miles. The embankments will be twice this length; that is, 1,260 miles. I have estimated that the sea wall at the mouth of the river could be built at $200,000 a mile, thus for both sides $400,000 a mile will be sufficient or the 140 miles from the deep sea to Kiangyin. For, in this part we have only the two embankments to deal with, which merely requires the tumbling of stones into the water until the pile is strong enough to hold the current to a directed course.

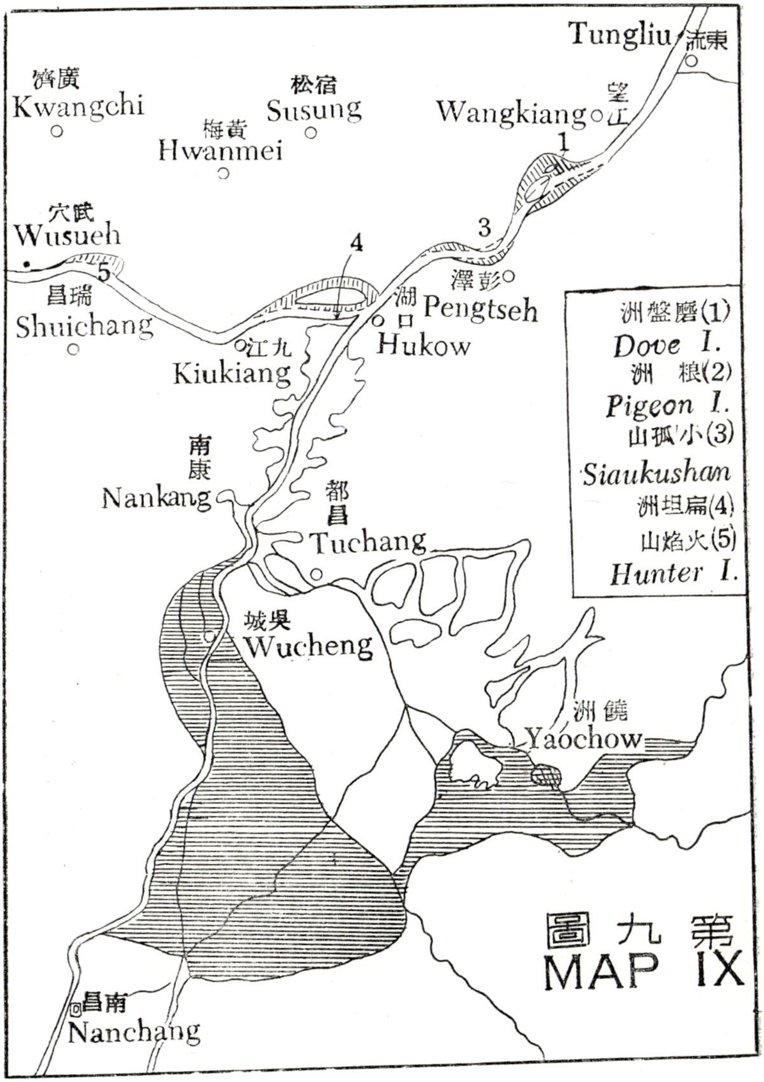

Tungliu 東流
廣濟 Kwangchi
宿松 Susung
黃梅 Hwanmei
Wangkiang 望江
武穴 Wusueh
瑞昌 Shuichang
九江 Kiukiang
湖口 Hukow
彭澤 Pengtseh
南康 Nankang
都昌 Tuchang
吳城 Wucheng
饒洲 Yaochow
南昌 Nanchang
1
3
4
5
磨盤洲(1)
Dove I.
糧洲(2)
Pigeon I.
小孤山(3)
Siaukushan
扁坦洲(4)
火焰山(5)
Hunter I.

第九圖
MAP IX

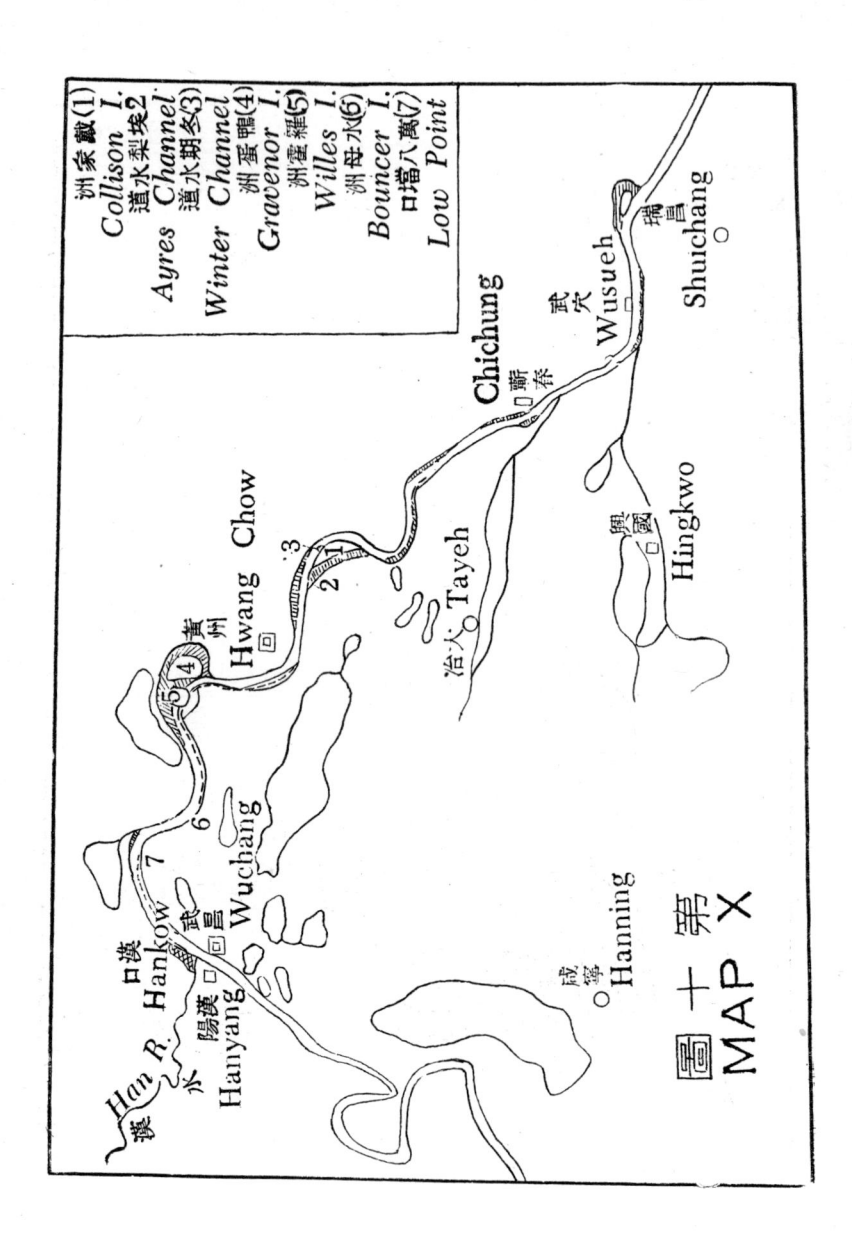

洲系戴(1) Collison I.
道水梨埃(2) Ayres Channel
道水期冬(3) Winter Channel
洲蛋鴨(4) Gravenor I.
洲堂維(5) Willes I.
洲母水(6) Bouncer I.
口擋八萬(7) Low Point

漢 Han R.
口漢 Hankow
陽漢 Hanyang
武昌 Wuchang
黃州 Hwang Chow
蘄菜 Chichung
冶大 Tayeh
武穴 Wusueh
興國 Hingkwo
蹄昌 Shuchang
諴寧 Hanning

第十圖
MAP X

As soon as these stone ridges on both sides of the river are formed, nature will do the rest to make the channel deep. The work for this part, therefore, is simple.

But the work for certain sections of the upper part of the river is more complicated as about fifty or sixty miles of solid land of from ten to twenty feet above water level and thirty to forty feet below have to be cut in order to straighten the river's course. Of this cutting and removing work, how much will have to be done artificially and how much can be done by nature, I leave to the experts to estimate. Excepting this, the other parts of this work, I think, cannot cost much more than $400,000 a mile. So that the whole work from the sea to Hankow, a distance of 630 miles will cost about $252,000,000, or let us say, including the unknown part, $300,000,000 for the completion of the entire project for the regulating of the Yangtze River. By this regulating of the Yangtze River, we secure an approach of 600 miles inland for ocean-going vessels into the very center of a continent of two hundred millions of people of which half or one hundred million is located immediately along 600 miles of the great water highway. As regards remuneration for the work, this project will be more profitable than either the Suez or Panama Canal.

Although we could not find means whereby the works above Kiangyin may be made self-paying as those of the sections below by the reclamation of land, profit from city building along the course of the river can be realized after the regulating work is completed.

In conclusion, I must say that the figures given concerning the harbor works and the Yangtze regulation are merely rough estimates which must be in the nature of the case. As regards the costs of building the rudimental dikes at the estuary of the Yangtze as well as along the dilating parts of the river, the estimation may seem too low. But the data on which I base my estimate are as follows: First, my own ogservation of the private enterprise of reclamation by building dikes at the Canton delta around my native village; second, the cheap stone that can be obtained at the Chusan Archipelago; third, the estimation of Mr. Tyler, Coast Inspector of the Maritime Customs for the blocking up of the North Channel at the upper end of Tsungming Island, where the narrowest part is about three miles. He says that a million taels or more is necessary for the work. Or, let us say, in round figures, five hundred thousand dollars (Mex.) a mile. This is two and a half times my estimate. Now, let us compare the difference. The three-mile channel at the upper end of Tsungming has an average depth of twenty feet of water, while in my project the sea wall or dikes will be built in water having an average of less than two thirds of this depth. Moreover, the work of blocking up the North Channel entirely at a right angle is many times more costly than that of building a rudimental dike of the same length in a parallel line with the current. Since five hundred thousand dollars are enough to block up cross-wise a mile of river twenty feet deep, two fifths of that sum should be quite sufficient to finance the work that I have projected. While writing this, I came across an article in the *Chicago Railway Review*, May 17, 1919, dealing with the same subject, which states that steel skeleton is a better and cheaper substitute for stone or other materials for building dikes and jetties in a muddy river like ours. Thus, by this new method, we may be able to construct embankments, with cheaper material than I have hitherto known. So, although the estimate which I have made may be somewhat low, yet it is not so far from correct as it seems at first sight.

PART III

The Construction of River Ports

The construction of river ports along the Yangtze between Hankow and the sea will be one of the most remunerative propositions in our development scheme. For this part of the Yangtse Valley is richest in agricultural and mineral products in China and is very densely populated. With the creap water transportation provided by the completion of the regulating work both sides of this water highway will surely become industrial beehives. And with cheap labor near by, it will not be a surprise if in the near future both banks will become two continuous cities, as it were, right along the whole extent of the river from Hankow to the sea. In the meantime a few suitable spots should be chosen for profitable city development. For this purpose I will start from the lower part of the river as follows:

  a. Chinkiang and North Side.
  b. Nanking and Pukow.
  c. Wuhu.
  d. Anking and South Side.
  e. Poyang Port.
  f. Wuhan.

A. CHINKIANG AND NORTH SIDE

Chinkiang is situated at the junction of the Grand Canal and the Yangtze. It was an important center of inland water traffic between the north and the south before the steam age. But it will resume its former grandeur and become more important when the old inland waterway is improved, and new ones are constructed. For it is the gateway between the Hoangho and Yangtze vallyes. Besides, by the southern portion of the Grand Canal, Chinkiang is connected with the Tsientang valley—the richest part of China. Thus, this city is bound to grow into a great commercial center in the near future.

In our regulation work of the Yangtze, we shall add a piece of new land, over six square miles, in front of Chinkiang. This land on the south side of the river will be utilized for city-planning for our new Chinkiang. On the north side, land should also be taken up by the state to build another city. The north side will be bound to outgrow that of the south for the whole of Hoangho Valley could only emerge into the Yangtze by waterway through this point. Docks should be built between here and Yangchow for accommodation of inland vessels, and modern facilities should be provided for transhipment between inland vessels and ocean-going steamers. This port should be made as a distributing center as well as a collecting center for the salt of the eastern coast. This, with the help of modern methods, will reduce transportation expenses. Stone or concrete bunds or quays should be built on both sides of the river and tidal jetties should be provided for train ferries. In time, when commerce grows, tunnels or bridges may be added to facilitate traffic of the two sides. The streets should be wide so as to meet modern demands. The water front and its neighborhood should be planned for industrial and commercial uses and the land beyond should be planned for residential purpose. Every modern public utility should be provided. In regard to the details of planning the city, I must leave them to the expert.

B. NANKING AND PUKOW

Nanking was the old capital of China before Peking, and is situated in a fine locality which comprises high mountains, deep water and a vast level plain—a rare site to be found in any part of the world. It also lies at the center of a very rich country on both sides of the lower Yangtze. At present, although ruined and desolate, it still has a population of over a quarter of a million. Once it was the home of many industries especially silk and now the finest satin and velvet are still produced here. Nanking has yet a greater future before her when the resources of the lower Yangtze Valley are properly developed.

In the regulation of the Yangtze I propose to cut away the town of Hsiakwan, so that the wharf of Nanking could be removed into the deep channel between Metsechow and the outskit of Nanking. This channel should be blocked up, thereby a wet dock could be formed to accommodate all ocean-going vessels. This point is much nearer the inhabited parts of the city than Hsiakwan. And the land between this projected wet dock and the city could form a new commercial and industrial quarter which would be many times larger than Hsiakwan. Metsechow in time, when commerce grows, may also be developed into city lots and business quarters. For the future development of Nanking the land within and without the city should be taken up at the present price under the same principle which I have proposed for the Projected Port at Chapu.

Pukow, opposite Nanking, on the other side of the river, will be the great terminus of all the railways of the great northern plain to the Yangtze. It will be the nearest river port for the rich coal and iron fields of Shansi and Honan, giving access to the lower Yangtze district and hence to the sea. As the great transcontinental trunk line to the sea whether terminating at Shanghai or at our Projected Port, would pass through this point, the construction of a tunnel under the Yangtze to connect Nanking and Pukow by rail at the same time when the cities are being constructed, will not be at all premature. This will at once make possible a through train journey from Shanghai to Peking.

Concrete or stone embankment should be built along the shore above and below the present Pukow point many miles in each direction. Modern streets should be laid out on the land within the embankment so as to be ready for various building purposes. The land on the north side of the river should be taken up by the state for public uses of this international development scheme on the same basis as at our Projected Ports.

C. WUHU

Wuhu is a town of 120,000 inhabitants and is the center of the rice trade in the lower part of the Yangtze. It is at this point that I propose to make an intake of the water which will go to flush the Whangpoo River at Shanghai, and which will form the upper end of a canal to the sea at Chapu. In the regulating work of the Yangtze the concave part above the junction of the Yangki Ho has to be filled up and the convex part of the opposite side has to be cut away. The junction of the projected canal and the river will be at about a mile or so below the Lukiang junction. The projected canal will run northeast to a point between the southeast corner of Wuhu city and the foot of the hill. There it joins the Yangki Ho and, following the course as far as Paichiatien, branches off in the northeastern direction. This gives Wuhu a southeast waterfront along the left side of the canal. New bunds should be built along both sides of the canal as well as alongside the Yangtze and at the junction of the canal docks for inland vessels should be constructed with modern plants for transhipment of goods. Wide streets should be laid out from the Bund of the Yangtze far into the inland following the direction of the canal. The bund alongside the Yangtze should be reserved for commercial purposes and those alongside the canal for factories. Wuhu is in the midst of a rich iron and coal field, so it will surely become an industrial center when this iron and coal field is properly developed. Cheap materials, cheap labor, and cheap foodstuffs are abundant at the spot waiting for modern science and machinery to turn them into greater wealth for the benefit of mankind.

D. ANKING AND SOUTH SIDE

Anking, the capital of Anhwei, was once a very important city but since its destruction by the Taiping war it has never recovered its former greatness. Its present population is about 40,000 only. Its immediate neighborhood is very rich in mineral and agricultural products. The great tea district of Liu-an and the rich mineral district in the southeastern corner of Honan province will have to make Anking their shipping port when railways are developed. In the Yangtze Conservancy work, the concave turn of the river in front and west of the city has to be filled up. This reclaimed land should be for the extension of a new city, where modern transportation plants should be built.

Eagle Point, on the south side opposite Anking should be cut away to make the river curve more gently and to give the channel a uniform width. A new city should be laid out at this point, for from here we command the vast tea districts of southern Anhwei and western Chekiang. The rich inland city of Hweichow, with the highly productive country around it, will have to make this port its shipping station. As Wuhu is the center of the rice trade these twin cities of Anking will be the centers of the tea trade. Like Wuhu, these twin cities are also situated in the midst of rich iron and coal fields which will assist them to become important industrial centers in the near future. So to build twin cities at this point of the river will be a very profitable undertaking.

E. THE POYANG PORT

I propose to construct a port at a point between the Poyang Lake and the Yangtze River. This will be the sole port of the Kiangsi province. Every city of this province is connected by natural waterways which, if improved, will become a splendid water transportation system. The province of Kiangsi has a population of 30,000,000 and is extremely rich in mineral resources. A modern port acting as a commercial and industrial center for the development of this resourceful province would be a most remunerative proposition in our project.

The site of the port will be on the west side of the entrance to the Poyang Lake and the right bank of the Yangtze. It will be an entirely new city built on new ground, part of which will be reclaimed from the shallow side of the lake. In the regulating work of the Poyang Channel, a training wall should be built from the foot of the Taku Tang Hill to Swain Point opposite to Stone Bell Hill of Hukow. A closed dock should be constructed within this training wall for the accommodation of inland water vessels. The city should be laid out on the triangular space formed by the right bank of the Yangtze, the left side of the Poyang Lake and the foot hill of the Lushan Mountain. This triangle is about 10 miles on each side, excellent for city development. The porcelain industry should be established here instead of at Kingteh Chen, for great damages often occur owing to the lack of transportation facilities, and to the necessity of transhipment for the export of the finished articles from the latter place. Modern plants on a large scale should be adopted for the manufacturing of cheap wares as well as fine articles in our projected Poyang Port, for here we shall have the greater advantage of collecting raw materials than at Kingteh Chen. Thus the concentrating of the various manufactures in an advantageous center will result in quickening the growth of our new city. This Poyang Port is bound to grow into one of the great commercial and manufacturing centers in China, judging from the possibilities of Kiangsi alone. It will not only be a great shipping port of the Yangtze but will also be a railway center between North and South China. Thus to develop this port on a large scale is quite justifiable from an economic point of view.

F. WUHAN

Wuhan signifies the three cities of Wuchang, Hankow, and Hanyang. This point is the headwater of our projected ocean passage, the pivot of the railway system of China Proper, and will become the most important commercial metropolis in the country. The population of these three cities is over a million and could be easily doubled or trebled if improvements would be made. At present, Hanyang possesses the largest iron works in China, and Hankow, many modern industries, while Wuchang is becoming a great cotton manufacturing city. Besides, Hankow is the trade center of Central and West China, and the greatest tea market we have. The provinces of Hupeh, Hunan, Szechuen, and Kweichow and a part of Honan, Shensi, and Kansu all depend upon Hankow as their only port in the outside world. When railways are developed in China, Wuhan will be still more important and will surely become one of the greatest cities in the world. So in planning the future city of Wuhan we must adopt for its development a scale as large as that of New York or London.

In the regulation of the Yangtze embankments, we have to reclaim the front of Hankow from the jetty of Lungwangmiao at the junction of the Han River right along the left bank to the point where the Yangtze turns eastward. This reclaimed space will be at an average of about 500 to 600 yards wide. This will narrow down the river at this part to give a uniform channel of 5 to 6 cables in width and to give the Hankow settlement a strip of valuable land along its waterfront. This will also help to pay a part of the expenses for city construction. The sharp bend of the Han River just before it joins the Yangtze should be straightened so as to make a gentler curve around Lungwangmiao Point and thus enable the currents of both rivers to flow in the same direction at their junction. The Hanyang embankment will follow pretty closely the present shore line but not beyond the iron works jetty. The wide space of the river above Wuchang city should be walled in to make a closed dock for inland water as well as ocean going vessels. Below Wuchang, an embankment parallel to that of the left side should be built so as to make the future city extend far below the present one. A tunnel should be constructed to connect both embankments at a point where the Kinghan railway makes its first turn when it comes to the Yangtze River. And another tunnel or bridge should be constructed between Hankow and Hanyang on one side and Wuchang on the other at the junction of the Han River and the Yangtze. Additional tunnels or bridges may be constructed at different points when the city grows larger in the future. All the outlying land of these trio-cities should be taken up on the same basis as at our projected seaports, so that private monopoly and speculation in land may be prevented, and that the unearned increment will go to the State to help the payment of capital and interest on the foreign loans which are to be made in this international development scheme.

PART IV

THE IMPROVEMENT OF THE EXISTING WATERWAYS AND CANALS

The existing waterways and canals in connection with the Yangtze may be enumerated as follows:

- a. The Grand Canal.
- b. The Hweiho.
- c. The Kiangnan Waterway System.
- d. The Poyang Waterway System.
- e. The Han River.
- f. The Tungting System.
- g. The Upper Yangtze.

A. THE GRAND CANAL

The Grand Canal connects with the Yangtze at a point opposite Chinkiang and runs northward right up to Tientsin, a distance of over 600 miles. We understand that a detailed survey of the Kiangpeh part of the canal has begun and the work of improving it will commence soon. In our project, I propose to substitute the Kiangpeh portion of the Grand Canal by the Yangtze outlet of the Hweiho.

B. THE HWEIHO

The Hweiho rises in the northwest corner of Honan and runs southeast and east to the north of Anhwei and Kiangsu. Its outlets have been sealed up in recent years so its water has accumulated in the Hungtse Lake and it depends upon evaporation as its only means of disposing the water. Thus in the heavy rainy season, it floods a vast extent of the country surrounding the lake and causes great misery to millions of people. So the conservancy of the Hweiho is a very urgent question of China to-day. Recently many investigations have been made and many plans proposed. Mr. Jameson, chief engineer for the American Red Cross Society, has proposed two outlets for the Hweiho: one following the old course of the Yellow River to the sea and another through Paoying and Kao-yu Lakes to the Yangtze. In this project I propose to follow Mr. Jameson's plan for the sea outlet only as far as the old Yellow River and for the Yangtze outlet only as far as Yangchow. When the sea outlet or north branch reaches the old Yellow River I will lead it across into the Yenho and follow the Yenho to its northern turn. From there, we cut across the narrow strip of land into the Kuanho which enters the sea at the nearest deep water line. This saves a great deal of work of excavating the old course of the Hoangho. When the southern branch reaches Yangchow, I propose to make the canal pass east of that city instead of west as Mr. Jameson proposed, so that its current will join the Yangtze in the same direction at the new curve below Chinkiang city.

Both of these outlets or branches of the Hweiho should be made at least twenty feet deep right along, so that coastal vessels from the north to the Yangtze could use them as passage instead of going round the Yangtze estuary, thus shortening the distance by about 300 miles. And with twenty feet depth for both outlets, the Hweiho and the Hungtse Lake would be well drained and the present bottom of the lake, which is sixteen feet above sea level would be converted into agricultural land at once. Thus 6,000,000 mow of land could be reclaimed according to the estimate of Mr. Jameson, from the Hungtse and the neighboring lakes. If twenty dollars a mow be taken for its value, a sum of $120,000,000 could be netted. Besides this direct profit to the Government there is an area of some 17,000 square miles of occasionally flooded land which would be made flood-proof so that normally we shall have two crops a year instead of two only in five years. That is to say, the 17,000 square miles or 10,880,000 acres will be made to produce five times more than at present. For instance, if the value of the gross production be estimated at fifty dolars an acre, then the total value would be $544,000,000 Mex. and five times this sum would amount to $2,720,000,000 Mex. What an enormous profit to the country!

C. THE KIANGNAN WATERWAY SYSTEM

This system comprises the South Grand Canal, the Whangpoo, the Taihu, and its connections. The most important improvement I intend to make here is to widen and deepen the Wuhu-Ihsing Waterway between the Yangtze and the Taihu, and from there to dredge a deep channel right through the Taihu to a point midway of the Grand Canal between Suchow and Kashing. At Kashing, divide it into two branches:—one following the Kashing Sunkiang Canal to Whangpoo, and the other, to the Projected Port at Chapu. This waterway between the Yangtze and the Whangpoo, before it reaches Shanghai, should be made as wide and deep as possible so as to make it carry sufficient water to flush the Shanghai harbor as well as to provide a shorter passage for inland water vessels between the Yangtze and the seaports. This waterway will act as silt carrier by which the Taihu and the various lakes alongside of it may be reclaimed in the future. Besides the main object for which this canal is assigned, the reclamation scheme and the local traffic would also add profit to it. This makes its remuneration doubly sure. As no accurate surveys of the shallow Taihu and other lakes and swamps could be obtained, the exact number of mow to be reclaimed could not be given here. But in a rough estimate I should say that the reclaimed space of the Kiangnan Lakes would be about the same in extent as those of Kiangpeh (the North of the Yangtze).

D. THE POYANG WATERWAY SYSTEM

This system drains the entire area of Kiangsi province. Every hsien, city, and important town is reached by waterway. Waterways are the only means of communication in this province as well as in all the provinces of Southeastern China, before the advent of railways. The lower part of the Kiangsi waterway system suffers the same irregularities as those of the lower Yangtze as both are on low land. So, to regulate it, a similar work as that for the Yangtze should be applied. The Poyang Lake should be divided by deep channels from the junction of each river, and these should join together to form larger channels and finally unite into one main channel at a point near Chuki and, running through the narrow part of the lake, join the Yangtze at Hukow. The sides of the deep channels should be lined with submerged stone ridges as high as the shallow part of the lake, whereby the channels would serve the purpose of draining as well as of navigation.

The shallow space beside those channels will be reclaimed into arable land in due time. So the work of regulating the Poyang channels will be well paid by reclamation.

E. THE HAN RIVER

This river is navigable for small crafts through its main body up to Hanchung in the southwest corner of Shensi; and through its branches up to Nanyang and Shekichen in the southwest corner of Honan. This navigable stream command quite a large area of watershed. The upper part, that is above Siangyang, is in mountainous country. From Siangyang to Shayang it is in a wide, open valley and below Shayang it runs into the Hupeh swamp.

To improve this river dams should be built above Siangyang in order to utilize water power as well as to make locks for larger crafts to ascend to the navigable point now navigable only for small crafts. Below Siangyang, where the river is very wide and shallow, rudimental dikes should be constructed of stones or piles in order to restrict its channel and to reclaim the shallow space on both sides by natural process. In the swamp, the river should be straightened and deepened. A new canal between the Han and the Yangtze at Shasi should be constructed to provide a shorter passage between Hankow and Shasi and beyond. This canal in the swamp should be open to the lakes along its course so as to let the silt-carrying water enter into them in the flood season, thus filling them up quicker.

F. THE TUNGTING SYSTEM

This system of waterway drains the whole province of Hunan and beyond. The most important branches are the

Siangkiang and the Yuankiang. The former runs through Hunan into the northeast corner of Kwangsi province and connects with the Sikiang system by a canal near Kweilin. The latter runs across the west border of Hunan into the eastern part of Kweichow province. Both could be improved for the navigation of large crafts. The canal between the Yangtze and the Sikiang watersheds should be reconstructed and modern locks should be provided in it as well as along the two waterways. Thus, vessels of ten feet draught may freely pass between the Yangtze and the Sikiang. The Tungting Lake should be drained by deep channels in the same manner as the Poyang Lake, and its shallow space reclaimed by natural process.

G. THE UPPER YANGTZE

I include the part from Hankow to Ichang also in the Upper Yangtze, because it is at Hankow that the ocean navigation ends, and the inland water communication begins. So, in dealing with the improvement of the Upper Yangtze, I will begin at Hankow. At present the Upper Yangtze is navigable for shallow draught steamers up to Kiating, a point about 1,100 miles above Hankow by river. If improvement be made farther on, then shallow draught steamers could navigate right up to Chengtu, the capital of Szechuen province, and the center of the richest plain in West China, about sixty miles up the Min River.

To improve the Upper Yangtze from Hankow to Yochow, the work is much similar to that of the lower part. The channel should be regulated by rudimental dikes. The concave embankments in sharp bends should be protected by stone or concrete; obstacles in midstream should be removed. The great loop, called the Farmer Bend, above Kinkow, should be cut through at the neck of Paichow, and the sharp point of Hanchin Kwang should be cut away to make the curve of the river more gentle.

The tortuous part of the Yangtze, north of the Tungting Lake, between Kinho Kow and Skipper Point, should be blocked up altogether and a new channel made through Tungting Lake, returning to the Yangtze by the Yochow Channel. This avoids the crooked passage and shortens the river course considerably. From Skipper Point to Ichang the dilatation should be restricted by dikes of stone or piling, and some sharp points of the shores should be cut away to make the curves more gentle.

The Yangtze River above Ichang enters the Gorges which run about a hundred miles up to the Szechuen depression, known as the Red Basin. This part of the river from Ichang right along to its source is confined by rocky banks, very narrow and deep, having an average depth of six fathoms and at some particular points even thirty fathoms. Many rapids and obstructions occur along its course.

To improve the Upper Yangtze, the rapids should be dammed up to form locks to enable crafts to ascend the river as well as to generate water power. Obstructions should be blasted and boulders removed. Thus, a ten-foot channel right along from Hankow to Chungking could be obtained so that through inland water transportation could be established from Chungking to Peking in the north and to Canton in the south, as well as to all navigable points in

China Proper all the year round. In this way, transportation expenses to the richest emporium in West China could be reduced hundredfold. The benefit to the people will be enormous and the encouragement to commerce will indeed be great.

PART V

The Establishment of Large Cement Works

Steel and cement are the basis of modern construction, and the most important factors of the material civilization of the present age. In the various projects of our development scheme, the demand for steel and cement will be so enormous that all manufacturing countries combined will not be able to supply the needs. Therefore, in our first program, I have proposed to establish large steel works in the rich iron and coal fields in the provinces of Shansi and Chili; so in this second program I propose to establish large cement works along the shores of the Yangtze River. The Yangtze Valley is exceptionally rich in materials for cement, —limestone and coal lying side by side at the water edge along the navigable channel from Chinkiang upward. Thus, local supplies could be created for local needs.

At present, there is one cement works at Shihuiyau near Hoangshikang at the upper reach. It is situated between a deep water wharf and a limestone hill. The limestone is so near by that it can be cut and shoveled into the kilns immediately. Between Hankow and Kiukiang there are many places possessing the same advantage. Below Kiukiang, there are also many such advantageous positions as Matang, Wushiki and many others between Kiukiang and

Anking. Between Anking and Nanking there are exceptionally good locations for putting up cement works such as Tatung, Tikang, and Tsaishisze, all these places being provided abundantly with limestone and coal and iron, lying side by side.

With the huge harbor works, city building, and embankment construction, the market for cement will be so great that a capital of one to two hundred million dollars should be invested for the supply. This work should be started gradually in accord with the acceleration of the other works of the general development so that one project will further the other, and over-production and waste of capital individually in any of the parts of the general scheme will be guarded against. This will help make each of them a profitable business by itself.

PROGRAM III

The main feature of the third program will be the construction of a great southern port which will complete the plan for three first-class seaports in China as proposed in the preliminary part of this International Development Scheme. Our Great Southern Port will naturally be Canton, which is not only the center of commerce in South China but also the largest city in all China. Until recent times it was the largest city on the coasts of the Pacific, and the center of commerce of Asia. With the development of China, Canton will surely resume its former importance. Around this southern metropolis I formulate the third program as follows:

 I. The Improvement of Canton as a World Port.

 II. The Improvement of the Waterway System of Canton.

 III. The Construction of the Southwestern Railway System of China.

 IV. The Construction of Coast Ports and Fishing Harbors.

 V. The Establishment of Shipbuilding Yards.

PART I

THE IMPROVEMENT OF CANTON AS A WORLD PORT

Canton's position as a seaport has been taken away by Hongkong since its cession to England after the Opium War. But as a commercial center of South China, Canton still holds its own, despite the advantages of deep-water harbor, the artificial improvements of Hongkong, and the political dominance of England. The loss of its position as a seaport is entirely due to the ignorance of the Chinese people who never made any combined effort to improve the welfare of the country, and also to the corrupt government and officials of the Manchu dynasty. Since the establishment of the Republic, the people have begun to awake very rapidly and many schemes have been suggested to make Canton a seaport. This awakening of the millions of Chinese has caused much apprehension to the Hongkong Government. The authorities of that colony have been doing their utmost to hinder every move to restore Canton as a seaport and try to nip every scheme in the bud. Of course, if Canton is improved and made into a world port, then all the services that Hongkong performs for her as a shipping stage would be dispensed with altogether. But a developed Canton and a prosperous China will recompense Hongkong in various ways a hundred times more than its present position as the monopolized ocean port of a backward and poor China. Just look at the port of Victoria in British Columbia, which was once the only seaport of West Canada as well as the Northwestern region of the United States, but it prospered very little then with an undeveloped hinterland despite its monopolistic character. Whereas as soon as the rival ports arose, Vancouver on its own side, and Seattle and Tacoma on the American side, all within the same distance as Hongkong is to Canton, all of them because of a developed hinterland prospered wonderfully, despite the keen competition between them as seaports. Thus, we see that competitive seaports like Vancouver, Seattle, and Tacoma instead of killing Victoria, as was one supposed by shortsighted people, have made it more prosperous than ever. Then, why doubt that a prosperous Canton and a developed China would not give the same result to Hongkong? This is but a natural outcome. Therefore, there should be no fear that a prosperors Canton and a developed China would be harmful to Hongkong as a free port. So, instead of doing the utmost as hitherto to hinder the development of Canton as a seaport, the Hongkong authorities should do their utmost to encourage such a project. Besides, the development of Canton and South China will benefit the English as a whole commercially a hundred times more than Hongkong can do at present. Although the local authorities of that crown colony do not see far enough to realize it, however, I believe that the great statesmen and captains of industries in the now mightiest empire of the world would surely see it. With this belief in my mind I feel quite safe in giving publicity to the scheme of my international development of Canton as a world port in South China.

Canton is situated at the head of the Canton Delta, which is formed by the junction of three rivers—the Sikiang or West River, the Peikiang or North River, and the Tungkiang or East River. The area of this delta is about 3,000 square miles and it has the most fertile alluvial soil known in China. The land yields three crops a year—two crops of rice and one crop of other products such as potatoes or beets. In silk culture, it gives eight crops every year. The most delicious fruits of many varieties are produced in this delta. This is the most thickly populated district of all China. Within this delta and its immediate neighborhood, more than half of the population of Kwangtung province is found. This is the reason why, despite the great productivity of this fertile delta, large quantities of foods have to be supplied by the surrounding country as well as by foreign imports. Before the age of machinery Canton for centuries was well known as an industrial center of Eastern Asia. The workmanship and handicraft of its people are still unequaled in many parts of the world. If machinery will be introduced in its industries under our international development scheme, Canton will soon recover its former grandeur as a great manufacturing center.

As a world port, Canton is in a most advantageous position. Being situated at the junction of three navigable rivers and at the head of the ocean navigation it is a pivot of inland water as well as ocean communication in South China. If the Southwestern railway system is completed, then Canton will be equal in importance to the two great ports in North and East China, in regard to transportation facilities. The ocean approach of Canton is generally deep excepting at two points which can be easily trained and dredged to enable modern liners to pass in and out at any hour. The deep water line of the ocean reaches up to Lingting Island, where the depth is from 8 to 10 fathoms. Above Lingting, the channel gets shallower (about 3 or 4 fathoms) and runs about 15 miles up to the Fumen Entrance. From this point the water becomes deep again (between 6 and 10 fathoms) right up to the Second Bar—a distance of 20 miles. At the Second Bar, the water is about 18 to 20 feet deep for only a few hundred yards. After crossing the Second Bar, the water becomes deep again for a distance of 10 miles averaging about 30 feet deep up to the First Bar which will be the city limit of our future Canton.

To improve the Approach to Canton, I suggest that two submerged training walls be built at the left side of Canton Estuary above Lingting Island—one from the shore to the head of the Kongsu Bank, and another from the end of the same bank to the head of the Lingting Bank. The first training wall will be 3 to 4 feet under water just at the same level of the bank. The second wall will be from 4 feet at one end to 16 feet at the other, which are the levels of the respective banks which it connects. (See (1) (3) Map XI.) It will cross a channel of 24 feet deep between them. These two walls together with the four-foot Kongsu Bank will act as one continuous wall and will direct the undercurrent which now runs between the left shore and Lingting Bank, into the middle part of the estuary, thus cutting a channel between the bar and the bank of the same name to meet the deep water on the west side of Lingting Island. On the right side of the Canton Estuary, a training wall should be built from the lower part of Fraser Bank in a southeasterly direction across the 24-foot channel into the Lingting Bar ending at the east edge of that bar. (See (2) Map XI.) Thus, with these submerged walls on both sides of the estuary to confine the undercurrent in the middle, a very deep channel can be formed to connect with the Fumen Entrance at one end and the Lingting trough at the other both of which are about 50 feet deep so that a thoroughfare from deep sea right up to the Second Bar of the Pearl River will be created.

These submerged sea walls taken together are about 8 miles in length and will be built only 6 to 12 feet from the bottom of the sea. The expenses will not be much while the acceleration of the natural reclamation process will be very great. Thus, the lands that will be formed on both sides by these walls will far more than repay the expenses of the work of building these walls.

To regulate the Approach of Canton, in that part of the Pearl River from the Fumen Entrance to Whampoa, I suggest that the East River Estuaries be concentrated in a single outlet by using the uppermost channel which joins the Pearl River at the lower point of Davids Island. The other outlets of the East River, which joins the Pearl River below the Second Bar, should be closed up by dams built to the height of the normal water level so as to permit them to serve as flood channels in the rainy season. By concentrating the whole volume of water of the East River above the Second Bar, a stronger current could be obtained to flush the upper part of this section of the river.

In the training works of this section, I propose that several jetties should be built as follows: First, a jetty from Elliot Island at point (A) to the farther side of Calcutta Shoal opposite the lower point of Parker Island. This will block the current between Elliot Island and Calcutta Shoal and divert it into the present 36-foot channel thus making it deeper by its natural force. Second, another jetty from Bolton Island, at point (B) to midstream terminating at the lower side of the Second Bar, on the right side of the river. Third, a jetty from the lower point of Pattinger Island at (C) to midstream terminating at the lower side of the same bar on the left side of the river. Thus the Second Bar would be flushed by the concentrated current created by these two jetties. The shallow bottom above these jetties should be dredged to the required

MAP XI

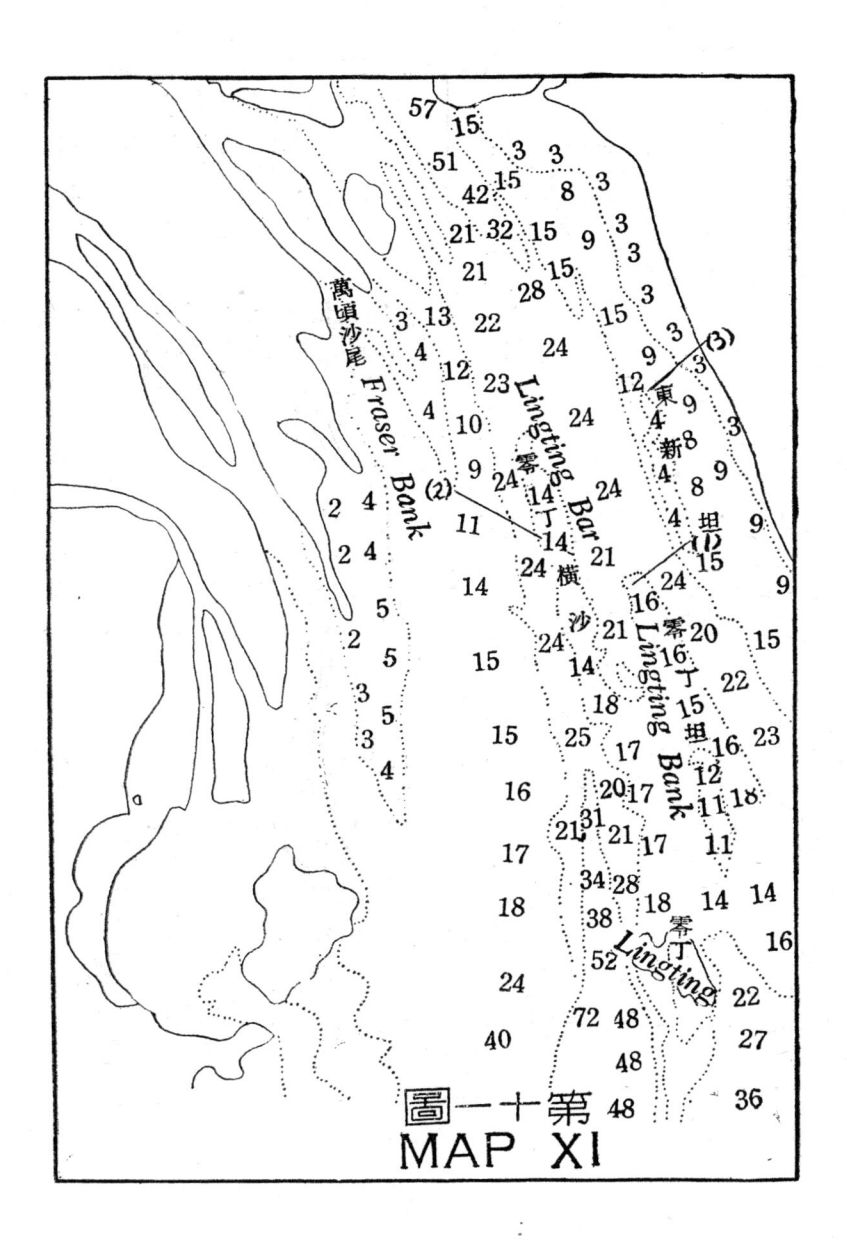

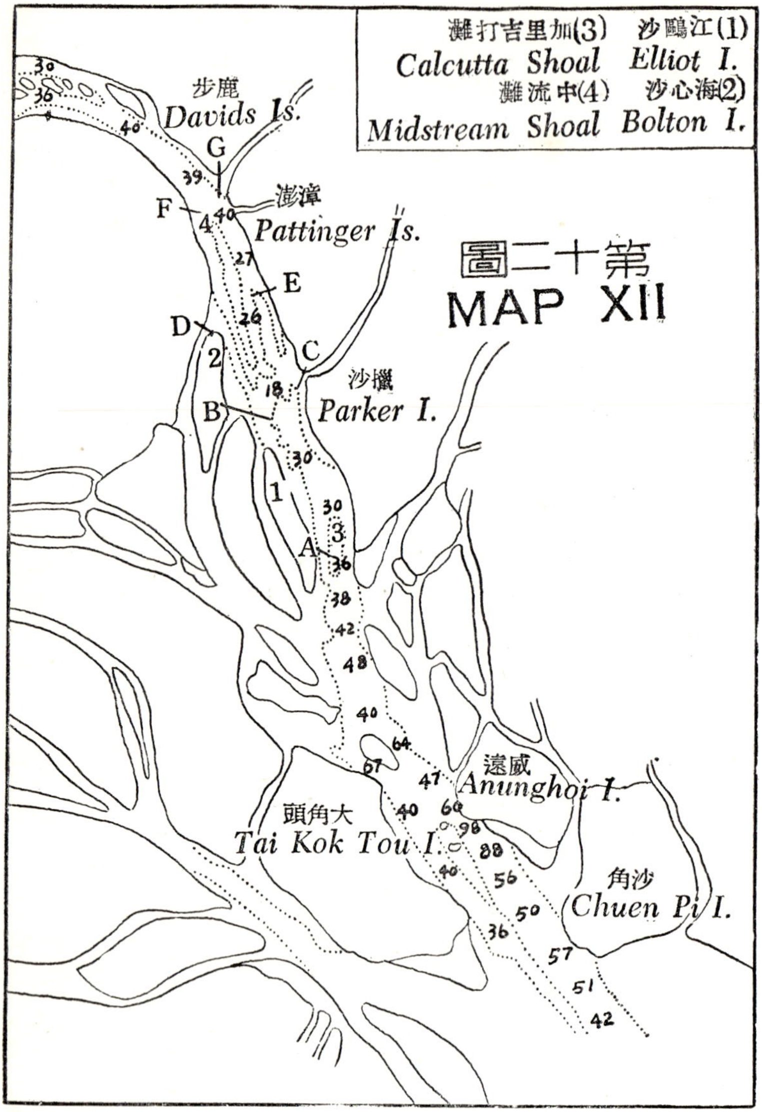
第十二圖
MAP XII
(1)江鷗沙
Elliot I.
(2)海心沙
Bolton I.
(3)加里吉打灘
Calcutta Shoal
(4)中流灘
Midstream Shoal
鹿步
Davids Is.
漳澎
Pattinger Is.
欖沙
Parker I.
威遠
Anunghoi I.
大角頭
Tai Kok Tou I.
沙角
Chuen Pi I.
A
B
C
D
E
F
G

depth. If a rocky bottom is found at this bar it should be blasted and removed, so as to give a uniform depth to the whole approach. Fourth, the channel between the right bank of the river and Bolton Island should be blocked up at (D). Fifth, a jetty from Pattinger Island at (E) to the head of the Second Bar Bank in midstream so as to cut off the current at the left side of the river and to increase the velocity in the middle channel. Sixth, a jetty from the right shore at (F) about midway between Danes Island and the Second Bar, should be built to the head of the Midstream Shoal so as to cut off the current at the right side of the river. And seventh, another jetty from the lower point of Davids Island at (G) to midstream opposite to the end of jetty (F). Jetties (G) and (F) will concentrate the current of the upper Pearl River while at the same time jetty (G) will also turn the East River current into the same direction as that of the Pearl River. (See Map XII.)

By these seven jetties, the current between Whampoa and Fumen could be controlled and the bottom of the river flushed to a depth of 40 feet or more, thus creating a thoroughfare for ocean-going steamers from the open sea right up to the city of Canton. These jetties taken together will be not more than 5 miles in length and mostly in very shallow water. After the building of these jetties, land will be rapidly formed between jetties along both sides of the channel by natural process. The reclaimed land alone will be quite enough to pay the expenses of constructing these jetties, aside from the fact that the main object of regulating the river and opening up a deep channel for ocean transportation will have been realized.

Having dealt with the approach to Canton, we may now take up the improvement of Canton City itself as a world port. The harbor limit of Canton will be at the First Bar. From there, the harbor will follow the deep water of Cambridge Reach and the water between Whampoa and Danes Island into American Reach. At this point it will cut through Actaeon Island to the south of Honam Island and follow the Elliot Passage to Mariners Island. From Mariners Island following the Fatshan Creek, a straight channel should be cut in a southwesterly direction to the Tamchow Channel. Thus, a new waterway will be made from the First Bar to Tamchow Channel, a distance of about 25 miles. This waterway will be the main outlet of the North River as well as a thoroughfare for the West River, and will also serve as the harbor of Canton. By conveying all the water of the North River and a part of that of the West River through this waterway, the current will be strong enough to flush the harbor to a depth of 40 feet or more. (See Map XIII.)

The new city of Canton will be extended from Whampoa to Fatshan, separated by the Macao Fort and Shameen Reaches. The section that lies east of this water should be developed into commercial quarters and that west of it into factory quarters. The factory section should be transected by canals connecting with the Fati and Fatshan creeks so as to give cheap transportation facilities to every factory. In the commercial section, tidal wharves with modern plants and warehouses should be provided. A bund should be built from the First Bar Island along the north side of the new waterway, the west side of Honam to connect with the bund of Shameen, and the northwestern

第三十圖
MAP XIII

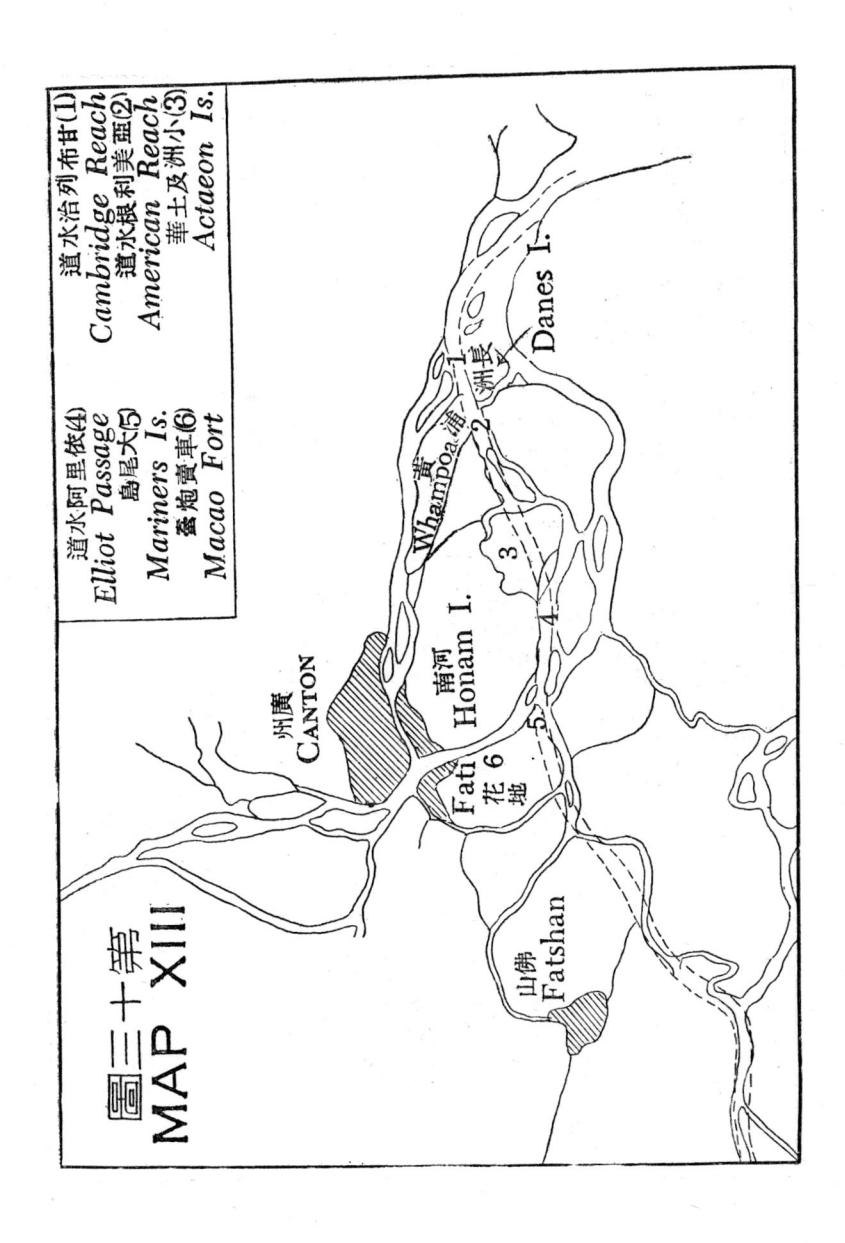

道水洽列布甘(1) Cambridge Reach
道水根利美亞(2) American Reach
華士及洲小(3) Actaeon Is.
道水阿里依(4) Elliot Passage
島尾大(5) Mariners Is.
蓋炮黃車(6) Macao Fort

廣州 CANTON
南河 Honam I.
花地 Fati
黃埔 Whampoa
長洲 Danes I.
佛山 Fatshan

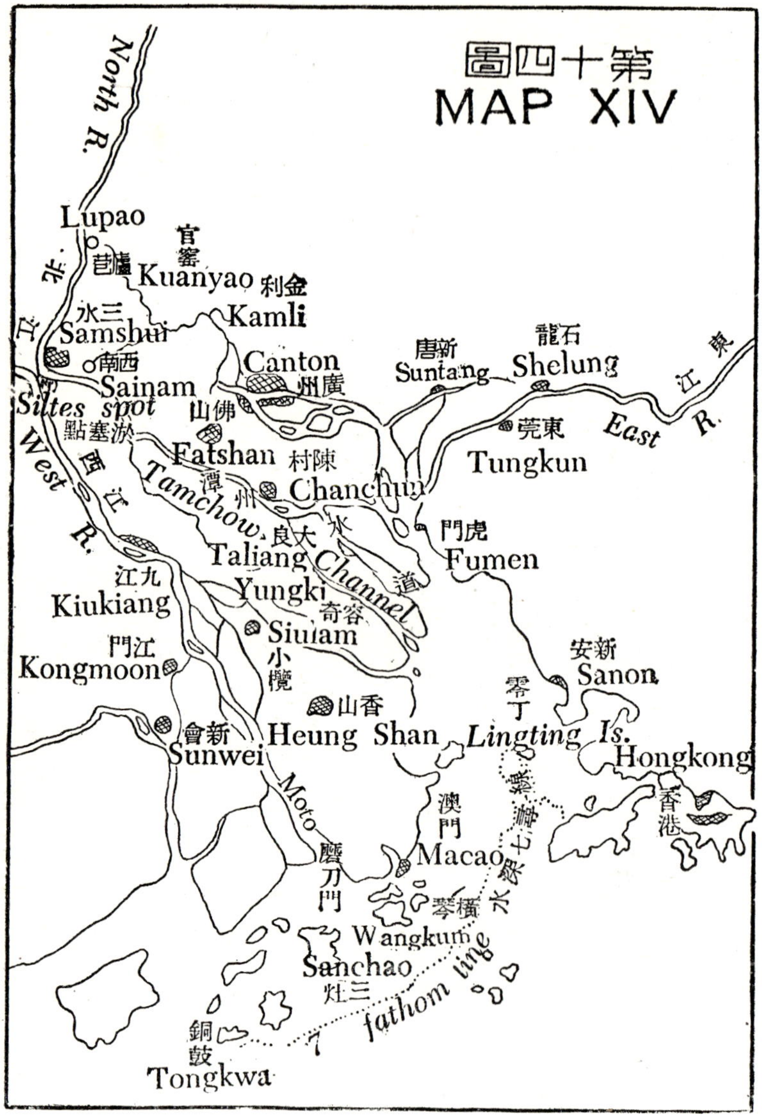
第十四圖
MAP XIV
North R.
Lupao
Kuanyao
Kamli
Samshui
Sainam
Canton
Siltes spot
Fatshan
West R.
Tamchow Channel
Chanchun
Taliang
Yungki
Siulam
Kiukiang
Kongmoon
Heung Shan
Sunwei
Moto
Macao
Wangkum
Sanchao
Tongkwa
7 fathom line
Suntang
Shelung
East R.
Tungkun
Fumen
Sanon
Lingting Is.
Hongkong

side of Canton city. Another bund should be built from above Fati along the east side of Fati Island to Mariners Island thence turning southwest along the left bank of the new waterway. The Front Reach, that is, the river between the present Canton city and Honam Island should be filled up from the upper point of Honam to Whampao for city building.

In regard to the question of remuneration, the development of Canton as a world port will be the most profitable undertaking of the kind in the International Development Scheme. Because, besides its commanding position as a commercial metropolis and its possession of advantageous facilities as a manufacturing center of South China, a modern residential city is in great demand in this part of the country. The well-to-do people and merchants of this rich delta as well as those retired Chinese merchants and millionaires abroad all over the world are very eager to spend their remaining days at home. But owing to the lack of modern conveniences and comforts they reluctantly remain in foreign countries. Thus to build a new city with modern equipments for residential purposes alone, in Canton, would pay splendidly. The land outside of Canton is at present about 200 dollars a mow. If the land marked off for the future city of Canton should be taken up by the State on the same basis as elsewhere in this International Development Scheme, immediately after the streets are laid out and improvements made, the price of land would rise from ten to fifty times its original value.

The landscape of the environment of Canton is exceptionally beautiful and charming. It is an ideal place for planning a garden city with attractive parks. The location of the city of Canton resembles that of Nanking but is of greater magnitude and beauty. It possesses three natural elements—deep water, high mountains, and vast extent of level land which furnish facilities for an industrial and commercial center and provide as well natural scenery for the enjoyment of man. The beautiful valleys and hills of the northern shore of the Pearl River could be laid out for ideal winter resorts and the high mountain tops could be utilized for summer resorts.

Within the city limits at the northwest corner, a rich coal field has been found. When the coal is mined and modern plants for generating electricity and producing gas are provided, then cheap electricity and gas could be had for transportation, for manufacturing, for lighting, heating, and cooking purposes. And so the present wasteful methods of transportation, and expensive fuels for manufacturing and cooking for the populous city of Canton can be done away with entirely. Thus great economic wonders could be wrought by such improvements. The present population of Canton is over a million and if our development plan is carried out, this city could grow in leaps and bounds within a very short time. The population will become greater than any other city and the profit of our undertaking will become correspondingly large.

PART II

THE IMPROVEMENT OF THE WATERWAY SYSTEM OF CANTON

The most important waterway system in South China is the Canton system. Besides this the others are not of much importance and will be dealt with elsewhere with their ports. In dealing with the Canton system of waterways, I have to divide it as follows:

      a. The Canton Delta.
      b. The West River.
      c. The North River.
      d. The East River.

A. THE CANTON DELTA

To improve the Canton Delta we have to consider the proposition from three points of view: First, the problem of flood prevention; second, the problem of navigation; and third, the problem of reclamation. Each of these problems affects the others so the solution of one will help that of the others.

First, the problem of flood prevention. The frequent repetition of floods in recent years has wrought great disasters to the people in the neighborhood of Canton. It has destroyed lives by the thousands and property by the millions. The part which suffers most is the country between Canton and Lupao, lying just immediately north of the Canton Delta. This fatal spot is, I think, created by the silting up of the main outlet of the North River immediately below Sainam. On account of this, the North River has to find its outlets through the West River by the short canal at Samshui and through two small streams one from Sainam, and another from Lupao. The former runs in a northeasterly direction and the latter in a southeasterly direction and they join at Kuanyao. From this point, the river takes a northeasterly course as far as Kumli, thence, turning southeast, passes the west suburb of Canton. Since the North River is silted up below Sainam, its channel above that spot is also getting shallower every year. At present the river above Samshui city is only about four or five feet deep. When the North River rises its water generally finds its way into the West River through the Kongkun Canal. But if the West River should rise at the same time, then there would be no outlet for the North River and its water would accumulate until it overflowed its dikes above and below Lupao. This would naturally cause the dikes to break at some point and allow the water to rush out and flood the whole country that is meant to be protected by these dikes. The remedy for the North River is to reopen the main outlet below Sainam and have the whole channel dredged deep from Tsingyuen to the sea. Fortunately, in our improvement of the navigation of the Canton Delta, we have to do the same thing; so this one work will serve two purposes.

The remedy for the West River is that the shallow part just at its junction with the sea between Wangkum and Sanchoo Islands should be trained by walls on both sides—a long one on the left, and a short one on the right—so as to concentrate the current to cut the river bed here to a depth of twenty feet or more. In this way, a uniform depth is secured, for after passing the Moto Entrance the West River has an average depth of 20 to 30 feet right along its whole course through this delta. With a uniform depth all the way to the sea, the undercurrent will run quickly and drain off the flood water more rapidly. Besides the deepening process, both shores should be regulated so as to give a uniform width to the channel. Mid-stream shoals and islands should be removed.

The East River Valley does not suffer so severely from floods as those of the other two rivers, the West and the North, and its remedy will be provided in the regulation of the river for navigation. This will be dealt with in that connection.

Second, the problem of navigation in the Canton Delta in connection with the three rivers. In dealing with this question we commence with the West River. In former days the traffic between the West River Valley and Canton always passed through Fatshan and Samshui, a distance of about 35 miles. But since the silting up of the Fatshan Channel below Sainam, the traffic has to take a great detour by descending the Pearl River southeastward as far as Fumen, then turn northwest into the Shawan Channel, then southeast into the Tamchow Channel, and then west into the Tailiang Channel and south into the Junction Channel and Maning Reach. Here it enters into the West River and runs a northwesterly direction up to Samshui Junction on this river. The whole journey covers a distance of about 95 miles, which compared with the old route is longer by 60 miles. The traffic between Canton and the West River Valley is very great. At present there are many thousands of steam launches plying between Canton City and the outlying districts, and more than half of that number are carrying traffic to and fro on the West River. Every boat has to run 95 miles on each trip whereas if the channel between Samshui and Canton is improved, the distance would be only 35 miles. What a great saving it will be!

In our project to improve the Canton Approach and Harbor, I suggested the draining of a deep channel from the sea to Whampoa and from Whampoa to Tamchow

Channel. We now have to prolong this channel from its Tamchow Junction up to Samshui Junction on the West River. This Channel should be made at least 20 feet deep so as to join the deeper water of the West River above the Samshui Junction. And the same depth should be maintained in the North River itself some distance above Samshui, so as to give facility for the navigation of larger vessels up the river when the whole waterway is improved.

To improve the East River for navigation in the Canton Delta we should concentrate the current of its estuaries into one single outlet by using the right channel which joins the Pearl River at Davids Island, thus deepening the channel as well as shortening the distance between Canton and the East River districts when the upper part of the river is improved.

Another improvement in the Canton Delta for navigation is the opening of a straight canal between Canton City and Kongmoon so as to shorten the passage of the heavy traffic between this metropolis and the Szeyap districts. This canal should begin by straightening the Chanchun Creek south of Canton as far as Tsznai. Then crossing the Tamchow Channel it should enter into the Shuntuck Creek and follow this creek to its end emerging into the Shuntuck Branch at right angles. From there, a new canal must be cut straight to the turn of the Tailiang Channel near Yungki, then the canal should follow this channel through Yellow Reach as far as the Junction Bend. Here another new canal must be cut through to the Hoichow Creek, then it should follow Kuchan Channel to the main channel of the West River, and crossing it enter into the Kongmoon Branch. Thus, a straight canal can be formed between Canton and Kongmoon. In order to understand the improvement of the Canton Delta more clearly see Maps XIV and XV.

Third, the problem of reclamation. A very profitable undertaking in the Canton Delta is the reclamation of new land. This process has been going on for centuries. Many thousands of acres of new land are thus being added to cultivation from year to year. But hitherto all the reclamation has been effected by private enterprise only, and there are no regulations for it. So sometimes this private enterprise causes great detriment to public welfare such as blocking up navigable channels and causing floods. A glaring case is the reclamation work just above the Moto Islands, which blocks more than half of the Main Channel of the West River. In the regulation of the West River, I propose to cut this new land away. In order to protect the public welfare, the reclamation work in this Delta must be taken up by the State and the profits must go to defray the expenses of improving this waterway system for navigation, as well as for the prevention of floods. At present, the area that can be gradually reclaimed is large in extent. On the left side of the Canton Estuary, the available area is about 40 square miles, and on the right side, about 140 square miles. On the estuaries of the West River from Macao to Tongkwa Island, there is an available area of about 200 square miles. Of the 380 square miles, about one fourth would be ready for reclamation within the next ten years. That is to say about 95 square miles could be reclaimed and put to cultivation within a decade. As one square mile contains 640 acres and one acre six mow, so 95 square miles will be equal to 364,800 mow. As cultivated land in this part of China generally costs more than fifty dollars a mow, so, if fifty dollars be taken as the average rate, the value of these 364,800 mow would amount to $18,240,000. This will help a great deal to defray the expenses of improving the waterway for navigation and for preventing floods in this Delta.

B. THE WEST RIVER

The West River is at present navigable for comparatively large river steamers up to Wuchow, a distance of 220 miles by water from Canton, and for small steamers up to Nanning, a distance of 500 miles from Canton, at all seasons. As for small crafts, the West River is navigable in most of its branches, west to the Yunnan frontier, north to Kweichow, northeast to Hunan and he Yangtze Valley by the Shingan Canal.

In improving the West River for navigation I shall divide the work into subsections as follows:

(1) From Samshui to Wuchow.

(2) From Wuchow to the junction of the Liukiang.

(3) Kweikiang or the North Branch of the West River from Wuchow to Kweilin and beyond.

(4) The South Branch from Shunchow to Nanning.

(1) *From Samshui to Wuchow.* This part of the West River is generally deep and does not need much improvement for vessels up to ten-foot draught excepting at a few points. The midstream rocks should be blasted and removed, and sand banks and dilating parts should be regulated by submerged dikes to secure a uniform channel

第十五圖 ―― 指示治水工程建堤及開鑿浚深之處

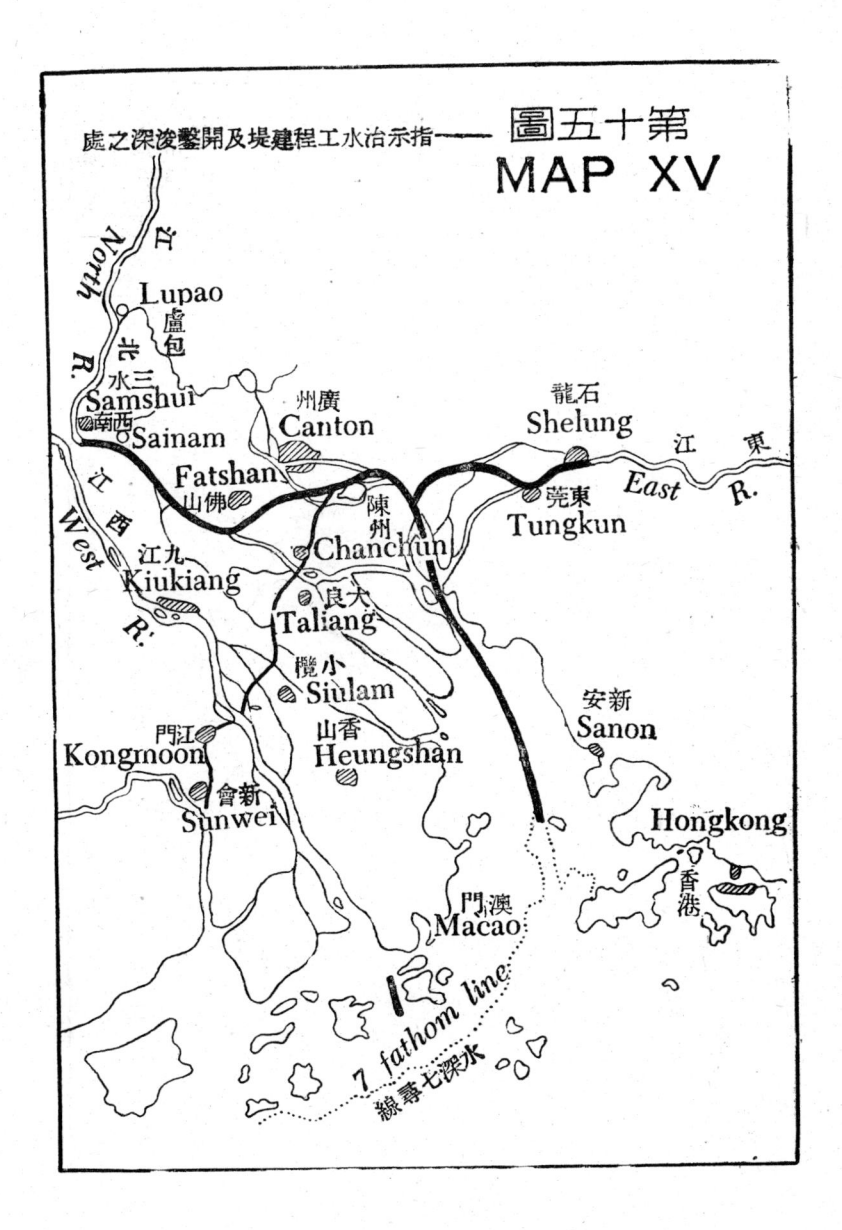

MAP XV

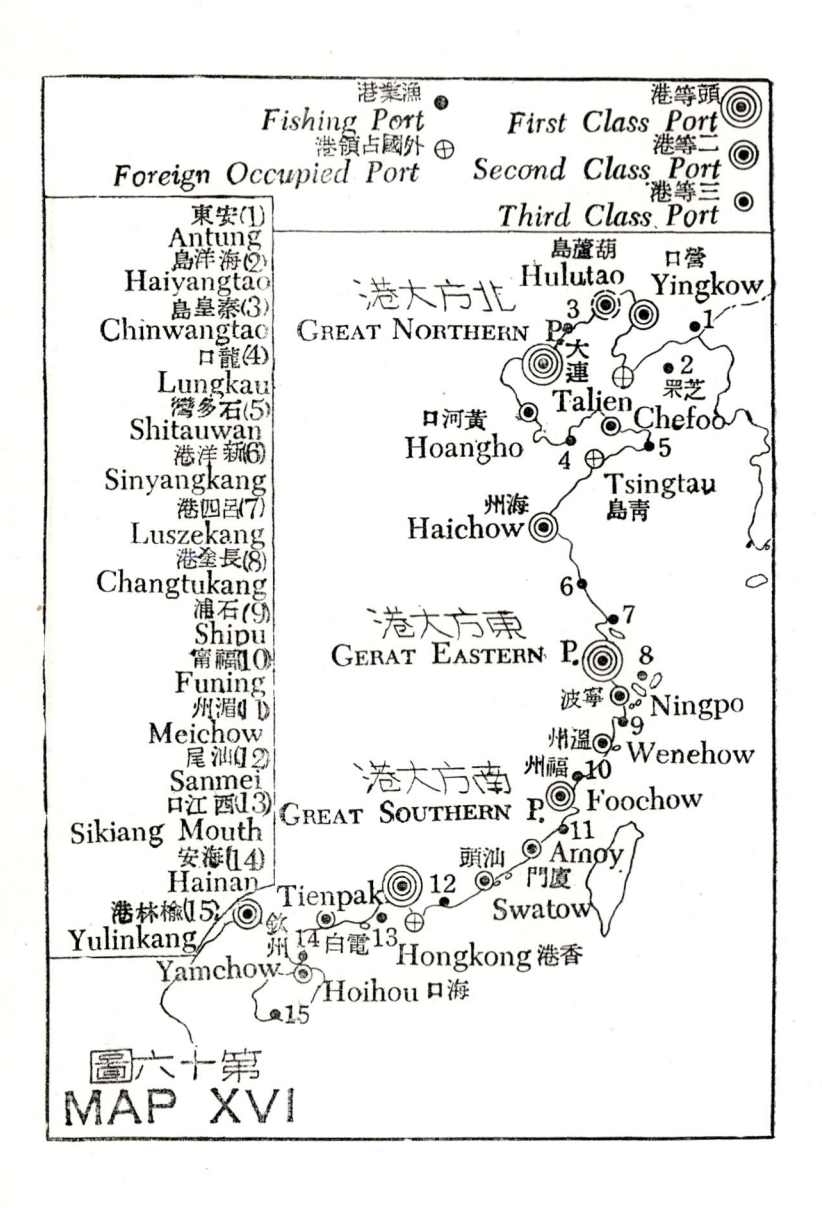

漁業港 Fishing Port
外國占領港 Foreign Occupied Port
頭等港 First Class Port
二等港 Second Class Port
三等港 Third Class Port

(1) 東安 Antung
(2) 海洋島 Haiyangtao
(3) 秦皇島 Chinwangtao
(4) 龍口 Lungkau
(5) 石多灣 Shitauwan
(6) 新洋港 Sinyangkang
(7) 呂四港 Luszekang
(8) 長壑港 Changtukang
(9) 石浦 Shipu
(10) 福甯 Funing
(11) 湄州 Meichow
(12) 汕尾 Sanmei
(13) 西江口 Sikiang Mouth
(14) 海安 Hainan
(15) 榆林港 Yulinkang

北大方港 Great Northern P.
葫蘆島 Hulutao
營口 Yingkow
大連 Talien
芝罘 Chefoo
黃河口 Hoangho
青島 Tsingtau
海州 Haichow
東大方港 Great Eastern P.
甯波 Ningpo
溫州 Wenchow
南大方港 Great Southern P.
福州 Foochow
廈門 Amoy
汕頭 Swatow
欽州 Yamchow
電白 (13)
香港 Hongkong
海口 Hoihou
Tienpak

第十六圖
MAP XVI

and to make the velocity of the current even, so that a stable fairway could be mantained all the year round. The traffic of this river would be sufficiently great to pay for all the improvements which we propose to make.

(2) From Wuchow to the Junction of the Liukiang. At this junction, a river port should be built to connect the deep navigation from the sea and the shallow navigation of Hungshui Kiang and the Liukiang which penetrate the rich mineral districts of Northwest Kwangsi and Southwest Kweichow. This port will be about fifty miles from Shunchow which is the junction of the Nanning branch of the river. So here we have only to improve a distance of fifty miles, for the improvement of the river between Shunchow and Wuchow will be included in the plan for the Nanning Port. Dams and locks would be necessary to make this part of the river navigable for ten-foot draught vessels. But these dams at the same time would serve the purpose of producing water power.

(3) Kweikiang or the North Branch of the West River from Wuchow to Kweilin and beyond. As Kweikiang is smaller, shallower and has more rapids along its course, so its improvement will be more difficult than that of the other parts of the waterway. But this will be a very profitable proposition in this Southern materway project, for this river not only serves the purpose of transportation in this rich territory but will also serve as a passage for through traffic beween the Yangtze and the West River valleys. The improvement should commence from the junction at Wuchow up to Kweilin, and thence upward to the Shingan Canal, then downward to the Siang River, and thereby connecting with the Yangtze River. A series of dams and locks should be built for vessels to ascend to the inter-

watershed canal and another series should descend on the other side. The expenses of building these two series of dams and locks could not be estimated until accurate surveys are made. But I am sure this project will be a paying one.

(4) From Shunchow to Nanning. This portion of the Yuhkiang is navigable for small steamers up to Nanning, the center of commerce in South Kwangsi. From Nanning small crafts can navigate through the Yuhkiang as far as the east border of Yunnan, and through Tsokiang as far as the north border of Tongking. If this waterway be improved up to Nanning, then it would be the nearest deep river port for the rich mineral districts of the whole southwest corner of China, which includes the whole province of Yunnan, a greater part of Kweichow and half of Kwangsi. The immediate neighborhood of Nanning is also very rich in minerals, such as antimony, tin, iron, coal and also in agricultural products. So to make Nanning the head of a deep water communication system will be a paying proposition. To improve the waterway up to Nanning, a few dams and locks along its course will have to be built for vessels of ten-foot draught to go up as well as for water power. The expense for this work cannot be estimated without detailed surveys but it would probably be much less than the improvement of Kweikiang from Wuchow to the Shingan Canal.

C. THE NORTH RIVER

The North River from Samshui to Shiuchow is about 140 miles long. The greater part of its course is confined in the hilly districts, but after it emerges from the Tsingyuen Gorge it comes into a wide, open country, which connects with the plain of Canton. Here the dangerous floods occur most often. Since the silting up of its proper outlet below Sainam, the North River from that point up to the gorge has become shallower every year, so the dikes at the left side, that is, on the side of the plain, often break thus causing the inundation of the whole plain above Canton. Thus the regulation of the river at this part has two aspects to be considered: First the prevention of flood and second, the improvement for navigation. In dealing with the first aspect nothing could be better than deepening the river by dredging. In the improvement of the Canton Approach and Harbor and also of the Canton Delta, we have to cut a deep channel right from the deep sea up to Sainam. In the improvement of the lower part of the North River, we have simply to continue the cutting process higher up until we have a deep channel, say 15 to 20 feet as far as the Tsingyuen Gorge, either by artificial or natural means. By this deepening of the bottom of the river, the present height of the dikes will be quite enough to protect the plains from being flooded.

In dealing with the second aspect, as we have already deepened the part of the river from Sainam to the Tsingyuen Gorge for flood prevention, we have at the same time solved the navigation question. It has now only the upper part to be dealt with. I propose to make this river navigable up to Shiuchow, the center of commerce as well as the center of the coal and iron fields of Northern Kwangtung. To improve the part above the gorge for navigation, dams and locks should be built in one or two places before a ten-foot draught vessel can ascend up to that point. Although this river is paralled with the Hankow-Canton Railway, yet if the coal and iron fields of Shiuchow are properly developed, a deep waterway will still be needed for cheap transportation of such heavy freight as iron and coal to the coast. So to build dams for water power and to construct locks for navigation in this river will be a profitable undertaking as well as a necessary condition for the development of this part of the country.

D. THE EAST RIVER

The East River is navigable for shallow crafts up to Laolung Sze, a distance of about 170 miles from the estuary at the lower point of Davids Island near Whampoa. Along its upper course, rich iron and coal deposits are found. Iron has been mined here since time immemorial. At present most of the utensils used in this province are manufactured from the iron mined. So to make a deep navigable waterway up to these iron and coal fields will be most remunerative.

To improve the East River for navigation as well as for flood prevention, I propose to start the work at the lower point of Davids Island as stated in the improvement of the Canton Approach. From here, a deep channel should be dredged up to Suntang, and a mile above that point a new channel should be opened in the direction of Tungkun city, by connecting the various arms of water between these two places and joining the left branch of the East River immediately above Tungkun city. All other channels leading from this new channel to the Pearl River should be closed up to normal water level so as to make these closed-up channels serve as flood outlets in rainy seasons. Thus by blocking up the rest of the estuaries of the East River, all the water would form one strong current which would dredge the river bottom deeper, and maintain the depth permanently. The body of the river should be trained to a uniform width right along its course up to tidal point, and above this point, the river should be narrowed in proportion to its volume of water. Thus the whole river would dredge itself deep far up above Waichow city. The railway bridge at the south side of Shelung should be made a turning bridge so as to permit large steamers to pass through it. Some sharp turns of the river should be reduced to gentle curves and midsteam obstacles should be removed. The portion of the river above Waichow should be provided with dams and locks so as to enable ten-foot draught vessels to ascend as near as possible to the iron and coal fields in the valley.

PART III

The Construction of the Southwestern Railway System of China

The southwestern part of China comprises Szechwan, the largest and richest province of China Proper, Yunnan, the second largest province, Kwangsi and Kweichow which are rich in mineral resources, and a part of Hunan and Kwangtung. It has an area of 600,000 square miles, and a population of over 100,000,000. This large and populous part of China is almost untouched by railways, except a French line of narrow gauge from Laokay to Yunnanfu, covering a distance of 290 miles.

There are great possibilities for railway development in this part of the country. A network of lines should radiate fan-like from Canton as pivot to connect every important city and rich mineral field with the Great Southern

Port. The construction of railways in this part of China is not only needed for the development of Canton but also is essential for the prosperity of all the southwestern provinces. With the construction of railways rich mines of various kinds could be developed and cities and towns could be built along the lines. Developed lands are still very cheap and undeveloped lands and those with mining possibilities cost almost next to nothing even though not state owned. So if all the future city sites and mining lands be taken up by the government before railways construction is started, the profit would be enormous. Thus no matter how large a sum is invested in railway construction, the payment of its interest and principal will be assured. Besides, the development of Canton as a world port is entirely dependent upon this system of railways. If there be no such network of railway traversing the length and breadth of the southwestern section of China, Canton could not be developed up to our expectations.

The southwestern section of China is very mountainous, except the Canton and Chengtu plains, which have an area of from 3,000 to 4,000 square miles each. The rest of the country is made up almost entirely of hills and valleys with more or less open space here and there. The mountains in the eastern part of this section are seldom over 3,000 feet high but those near the Tibetan frontier generally have an altitude of 10,000 feet or more. The engineering difficulties in building these railways are much greater than those of the northwestern plain. Many tunnels and loops will have to be constructed and so the construction costs of the railway per mile will be greater than in other parts of China.

DEVELOPMENT OF CHINA

With Canton as the terminus of this system of railroads, I propose that the following lines be constructed:

a. The Canton-Chungking line via Hunan.
b. The Canton-Chungking line via Hunan and Kweichow.
c. The Canton-Chengtu line via Kweilin and Luchow.
d. The Canton-Chengtu line via Wuchow and Suifu.
e. The Canton-Yunnanfu-Tali-Tengyueh line ending at the Burma border.
f. The Canton-Szemao line.
g. The Canton-Yamchow line ending at Tunghing, on the Annam border.

A. THE CANTON-CHUNGKING LINE VIA HUNAN

This line will start from Canton and follow the same direction as the Canton-Hankow line as far as the junction of the Linkiang with the North River. From that point the railroad turns into the valley of Linkiang, and follows the course of the river upward above the city of Linchow. There it crosses the watershed between the Linkiang and the Taokiang and proceeds to Taochow, Hunan. Thence it follows the Taokiang to Yungchow, Paoking, Sinhwa, and Shenchow, and up to Peiho across the boundary of Hunan into Szechwan by Yuyang. From Yuyang the line proceeds across the mountain to Nanchuen, thence to Chungking after crossing the Yangtze. This railway which has a total length of about 900 miles passes through a rich mineral and agricultural country. In the Linchow district north of Kwangtung, rich coal, antimony, and wolfram deposits are found; in southwestern Hunan, tin, antimony, coal, iron, copper and silver; and at Yuyang, east of Szechwan, antimony and quicksilver. Among agricultural products found along this line we may mention sugar, groundnuts, hemp, tung oil, tea, cotton, tobacco, silk, grains, etc. There is also an abundance of timber, bamboo and various kinds of forest products.

B. THE CANTON-CHUNGKING LINE VIA HUNAN AND KWEICHOW

This line is about 800 miles in length, but as it runs in the same track with line (a) from Canton to Taochow, a distance of about 250 miles, it leaves only 550 miles to be accounted for. This line, therefore, actually begins at Taochow, Hunan, and goes through the northeastern corner of Kwangsi passing by Chuanchow, and then through the southwestern corner of Hunan passing by Chengpu and Tsingchow. Thence it enters into Kweichow by Sankiang and Tsingkiang and crosses a range of hill to Chengyuan. From Chengyuan this line has to cross the watershed between Yuan Kiang and Wukiang to Tsunyi. From Tsunyi it will follow the trade route which leads to Kikiang and then crosses the Yangtze by the same bridge as line (a) to Chungking. This railway will also pass through rich mineral and timber districts.

C. THE CANTON-CHENGTU LINE VIA KWEILIN AND LUCHOW

This line is about 1,000 miles long. It runs from Canton directly west to Samshui, where it crosses the North River to the mouth of Suikong. Then, it ascends the valley of the same name to Szewui and Kwongning. Next, it enters into Kwangsi at Waisap, thence to Hohsien and Pinglo. From there it follows the course of the Kweikiang up to Kweilin. Thus the rich iron and coal fields that lie between these two provincial capitals, Canton and Kweilin, will be tapped. From Kweilin the road turns west to Yungning and then proceeds to follow the Liukiang valley into Kweichow province at Kuchow. From Kuchow it goes to Tukiang and Pachai and following the same valley it crosses a range of hills into Pingyueh, thence it goes across the Yuankiang watershed into the Wukiang valley at Wengan and Yosejen. From Yosejen it follows the trade route through Luipien hills to Jenhwai, Chishui, and Nachi. Then it crosses the Yangtzekiang to Luchow. From Luchow, it runs through Lungchang, Neikiang, Tzechow, Tseyang and Kienchow to Chengtu. The last part of the line traverses very rich and populous districts of the famous Red Basin of Szechwan province. The middle portion of this line between Kweilin and Luchow lies in a very rich mineral country which possesses great possibilities for further development. This line will open up a thinly populated part for the crowded districts at both ends of the line.

D. THE CANTON-CHENGTU LINE VIA WUCHOW AND SUIFU

This line is about 1,200 miles in distance. It commences at the west end of the Samshui bridge which crosses the North River at that point for line (c), and following the left bank of the West River enters the Shiuhing Gorge to the Shiuhing city. It passes Takhing, Wuchow, and Tahwang along the same bank. While the river here turns southwestwards the line turns northwestwards to Siangchow and then crosses Liukiang to Liuchow and Kingyuan. Then it goes to Szegenhsien and across the Kwangsi and Kweichow border to Tushan and Tuyun. From Tuyun the line turns more westerly to Kweiyang, the capital of Kweichow Province. Next, it proceeds to Kiensi and Tating and then leaving the Kweichow border at Pichieh it enters Yunnan at Chenhiung. Turning northward to Lohsintu and crossing the Szechwan border at that point, it proceeds to Suifu. From Suifu the road follows the course of the Minkiang, passes by Kiating and enters the Chengtu plain to Chengtu, the capital of Szechwan. This line runs from one densely populated district to another and passes through a wide strip of thinly populated and undeveloped country in the middle. Along its course many rich iron and coal fields, silver, tin, antimony, and other valuable metal deposits are found.

E. The Canton-Yunnanfu-Tali-Tengyueh Line

This line is about 1,300 miles in length from Canton to the Burma border at Tengyueh. The first 300 miles of the line from Canton to Tahwang will be the same as line (d). From the Tahwang junction this line branches off to Wusuan and following in a general way the course of the Hungshui Kiang passes through Tsienkiang and Tunglan. Then it cuts across the southwestern corner of Kweichow province passing by Sinyihsien and thence enters Yunnan province at Loping and by way of Luliang to Yunnanfu, the capital of the province. From Yunnanfu this line runs through Tsuyung to Tali, then turns southwestwards to Yungchang and Tengyueh ending at the Burma border.

At Tunglan, near the Kweichow border in Kwangsi, a branch line of about 400 miles should be projected. This line should follow the Pepan Kiang valley, up to Kotuho, and Weining. Thence it enters Yunnan at Chaotung, and crosses the Yangtze River at Hokeow, where it enters Szechwan. Crossing the Taliang mountain, it goes to Ningyuan. This branch line taps the famous copper field between Chaotung and Ningyuan, the richest of its kind in China.

The main line running through the length of Kwangsi and Yunnan from east to west, will be of international importance, for at the frontier it will join the Rangoon Bhamo line of the Burmese Railway System. It will be the shortest road from India to China. It will bring the two populous countries nearer to each other than now. By the new way the journey can be made in a few days, whereas by the present sea-route it takes as many weeks.

F. THE CANTON-SZEMAO LINE

This line to the border of Burma is about 1,100 miles long. It starts from south of Canton, passes Fatshan, Kunshan, and crosses the West River from Taipinghu to Samchowhu. Thence it proceeds to Koming, Sinhing, and Loting. After passing Loting it crosses the Kwangsi border at Pingho, and proceeds to Junghsien and then westward, crossing the Yukiang branch of the West River, to Kweihsien. Thence it runs north of Yukiang to Nanning. At Nanning a branch line of 120 miles should be projected. Following the course of the Tsokiang it goes to Lungchow where it turns southward to Chennankwan on the Tongking border to join the French line at that point. The main line from Nanning proceeds in the same course as the upper Yukiang to Poseh. Then it crosses the border into Yunnan at Poyai, and by way of Pamen, Koukan, Tungtu and Putsitang to Amichow, where it crosses the French Laokay-Yunnan line. From Amichow it proceeds to Linanfu, Shihping and Yuankiang where it crosses the river of the same name. Thence it passes through Talang, Puerhfu and Szemao and finally ends at the border of Burma near the Mekong River. This line taps the rich tin, silver, and antimony deposits of south Yunnan and Kwangsi, while rich iron and coal fields are found right along the whole line. Gold, copper, mercury, and lead are also found in many places. As regards agricultural products, rice and groundnuts are found in great abundance, also camphor, cassia, sugar, tobacco, and various kinds of fruits.

G. THE CANTON-YAMCHOW LINE

This line is about 400 miles long measuring from the west end of the Sikiang bridge. Starting from Canton it runs on the tracks of line (f) as far as the farther side of the bridge over the West River. Thence it branches off to the southwest to Hoiping and Yanping, and by way of Yeungchun to Kochow and Fachow. At Fachow, a branch line of 100 miles should be projected to Suikai, Luichow and Haian on the Hainan Straits where, by means of a ferry, it connects with Hainan Island. The mainline continues from Fachow westward to Sheshing, Limchow, Yamchow and ends on the Annam border at Tunghing, where it may connect with a French line to Haiphong. This line is entirely within the Kwangtung province. It passes through a very populous and productive country. Coal and iron are found along the whole line, while gold and antimony, in some parts. Agricultural products, as sugar, silk, camphor, ramie, indigo, groundnuts, and various kinds of fruits are raised here.

The total length of this system as outlined above is about 6,700 miles. In addition there will be two connecting lines between Chengtu and Chungking; another from east of Tsunyi on line (b) southward to Wengan on line (c); another from Pingyueh on line (c) to Tuyun on line (d); another from the border of Kweichow on line (d) through Nantan and Noti to Tunglan on line (e), thence through Szecheng to Poseh on line (f). These connecting lines total about 600 miles. So the grand total will be about 7,300 miles.

This system will be intersected by three lines. First, the existing French line from Laokay to Yunnanfu with a projected line from Yunnanfu to Chungking crosses line (f) at Amichow, line (e) at Weining, line (d) at Suifu, line (c) at Luchow, and meets lines (a) and (b) at Chungking. Second, the projected British line from Shasi to Sinyi crosses line (a) at Shenchow, line (b) at Chenyuen, line (c) at Pingyueh, line (d) at Kweiyang and a branch of line (e) at a point west of Yungning. Third, the projected American line from Chuchow to Yamchow crosses line (a) at Yungchow, line (b) at Chuanchow, line (c) at Kweilin, line (d) at Liuchow, line (e) at Tsienkiang, line (f) at Nanning, and meets line (g) at Yamchow. Thus, if this system and the three projected French, British, and American lines are completed, Southwestern China would be well provided with railway communications.

All these lines will run through the length and breadth of a vast mineral country, in which most of the essential and valuable metals of the world are found. There is no place in the world which possesses as here so many varieties of rare metals, such as wolfram, tin, antimony, silver, gold, and platinum and at the same time so richly provided with the common but essential metals, such as copper, lead, and iron. Furthermore, almost every district in this region is abundantly provided with coal, so much so that there is a common saying: "Mu mei pu lih cheng," that is, "Nobody would build a city where there is no coal underneath." The idea was that in case of a siege those within the city might obtain fuel from under the ground. In Szechuan, petroleum and natural gas are also found in abundance.

Thus, we see that this Southwestern Railway System for the development of mineral resources in the mountainous regions of Southwestern China is just as important as the Northwestern Railway System is for the development of agricultural resources in the vast prairies of Mongolia and Turkestan. These railway systems are a necessity to the Chinese people and a very profitable undertaking to foreign capitalists. They are of about equal length, viz.—about 7,000 miles. The cost per mile of the Southwestern System will be at least twice that of the Northwestern System, but the remunration from the development of mineral resources will be many times that from the development of agricultural resources.

PART IV

THE CONSTRUCTION OF COAST PORTS AND FISHING HARBORS

After planning the three world ports on the coast of China, it is time for me to go on and deal with the development of second- and third-class seaports and fishing harbors along the whole coast in order to complete a system of seaports for China. Recently, my projected plan of the Great Northern Port was so enthusiastically received by the people of Chili Province that the Provincial Assembly has approved the project and decided to carry it out at once as a provincial undertaking. For this object, a loan of $40,000,000 has been voted. This is an encouraging sign and doubtless the other projects will be taken up sooner or later by either the provinces or the Central Government, when the people begin to realize their necessity. I propose that four second-class seaports and nine third-class seaports and numerous fishing harbors should be constructed.

The four second-class seaports will be arranged so as to be placed in the following manner: one on the extreme north, one on the extreme south, and the other two midway between the three great world ports.

I shall deal with them according to the order of their future importance as follows:

    a.   Yingkow.
    b.   Haichow.
    c.   Foochow.
    d.   Yamchow.

A. YINGKOW

Yingkow is situated at the head of the Liaotung Gulf and was once the only seaport of Manchuria. Since the improvement of Talien as a seaport, the trade of Yingkow has dwindled and lost half of its former business. As a seaport, Yingkow has two disadvantages, first, the shallowness of its approach from the sea and second, the blocking up by ice for several months in winter. Its only advantages over Talien is that it is situated at the mouth of the Liaoho and has inland water communication throughout the Liao valley in south Manchuria. The half of the former trade that it still holds at present against Talien is entirely due to the inland water facility. To make Yingkow outmatch Talien again in the future and become first in importance after the three great world ports, we must improve its inland water communication, as well as deepen its approach from the sea. In regard to the improvement of the approach work similar to the improvement of the Canton Approach should be adopted. Besides the construction of a deep channel, about twenty feet in depth, reclamation work should be carried out at the same time. For, the shallow and extensive swamp at the head of the Liaotung Gulf could be turned into rice-producing land from which great profit could be derived. Regarding the inland water communication, not only the water system in the Liao valley but also the Sungari and the Amur Systems have to be improved. The most important work is the construction of a canal to connect these systems and this I shall now discuss in the next paragraph.

The Liaoho-Sungari Canal is the most important factor in the future prosperity of Yingkow. It is by this canal only that this port can be made the most important of the second-class seaports in China and further the vast forest lands, the virgin soil and the rich mineral resources of North Manchuria can be connected by water communication with Yingkow. So this canal is all important for Yingkow, without which Yingkow as a seaport could at most hold her present position, a town of 60,000 to 70,000 inhabitants and an annual trade of $30,000,000 to $40,000,000 only and could never gain a place as the first of the second-class seaports in China. This canal can be cut either south of Hwaiteh in a line parallel to the South Manchurian Railway between Fan Kia Tun and Sze Tung Shan, a distance of less than ten miles, or north of Hwaiteh in a line between Tsing-shan-pao and Kaw-shan-tun, a distance of about fifteen miles. In the former case the canal is shorter but it makes the waterway as a whole longer, while in the latter case, the canal is about twice as long but it makes the waterway as a whole shorter between the two systems. In either line, there are no impassable physical obstacles. Both lines are on the plain but the elevation of the one may be higher than that of the other, which is the only factor that will determine the choice between the two. If this canal is constructed, then the rich provinces of Kirin and Heilungkiang and a portion of Outer Mongolia will be brought within direct water communication with China Proper. At present, all water traffic has to go by way of the Russian Lower Amur, then round a great detour of the Japan Sea before reaching China Proper. This canal will not only be a great necessity to Yingkow as a seaport, but will also have a great bearing on the whole Chinese nation economically and politically. With the Liaoho-Sungari Canal completed Yingkow will be the grand terminus of the inland waterway system of all Manchuria and Northeastern Mongolia; and with the approach from the sea deepened it will also be a seaport next in importance only to the three first-class world ports.

B. HAICHOW

Haichow is situated on the eastern edge of the central plain of China. This plain is one of the most extensive and fertile areas on earth. As a seaport, Haichow is midway between the two great world ports along the coast line; namely the Great Northern and the Great Eastern Ports.

It has been made as the terminus of the Hailan railway, the trunk line of central China from east to west. Haichow also possesses the facility of inland water communication. If the Grand Canal and the other waterway systems are improved, it will be connected with the Hoangho Valley in North China, the Yangtze Valley in Central China, and the Sikiang Valley in South China. Its deep sea approach is comparatively good, being the only spot along the 250 miles of the North Kiangsu coast that could be reached by ocean steamers to within a few miles of the shore. To make Haichow a seaport for 20 feet draught vessels, the approach has to be dredged for many miles from the mouth of the river before the four fathom line could be reached. Although possessing better advantages than Yingkow, in being ice free, Haichow, as a second-class seaport, has to be content to take a second place after Yingkow, because she does not have as vast a hinterland as Yingkow, nor such a monopolistic position in regard to inland water communication.

C. FOOCHOW

Foochow, the capital of Fukien Province, ranks third among our second-class seaports. Foochow is already a very large city, its inhabitants being nearly a million. It is situated at the lower reach of the Min River, about 30 miles from the sea. The hinterland of this port is confined to the Min Valley with an area of about 30,000 square miles. The territory beyond this valley will be commanded by other coast or river ports, so the area commanded by this port is much smaller than that by Haichow. Consequently, it could be given only the third place in the category of second-class seaports. The Foochow approach from the Outer Bar to Kinpei Entrance is very shallow. After this Entrance is passed, the river is confined on both sides by high hills and becomes narrow and deep right up to Pagoda Anchorage.

I propose that a new port should be constructed at the lower part of Nantai Island. For here land is cheap and there will be plenty of room for modern improvement. A locked basin for shipping could be constructed at the lower point of Nantai Island, just above Pagoda Anchorage. The left branch of the Min River above Foochow City should be blocked up so as to concentrate the current to flush the harbor at the south side of Nantai. The blocked-up channel on the north side of that island should be left to be reclaimed by natural process or may be used as a tidal basin to flush the channel below Pagoda Anchorage, if it is found necessary. The upper Min River must be improved as far as possible for inland water traffic. Its lower reach from Pagoda Anchorage to the sea must be trained and regulated to secure a through channel of 30 feet or more to the open sea. Thus Foochow could also be made a calling port for ocean liners that ply between the world ports.

D. YAMCHOW

Yamchow is situated at the head of Tongking Gulf in the extreme south of the China Coast. This city is about 400 miles west of Canton—the Great Southern Port. All the districts lying west of Yamchow will find their way to the sea by this port 400 miles shorter than by Canton. As sea transportation is commonly known to be twenty times cheaper than rail transportation, the shortening of a distance of 400 miles to the sea means a great deal economically to the provinces of Szechuan, Yunnan, Kweichow, and a part of Kwangsi. Although Nanning, an inland water port, lying northwest of Yamchow, is much nearer to the hinterland than Yamchow, yet it could not serve this hinterland as a seaport. So all the direct import and export trade will find Yamchow the cheapest shipping stage.

To improve Yamchow as a seaport the Lungmen River should be regulated in order to secure a deep channel to the city, and the estuary should be deepened by dredging and training to provide a good approach to the port. This port has been selected as the terminus of the Chuchow Yamchow Railway (Chu-Kin line) which will run from Hunan through Kwangsi into Kwangtung. Although the hinterland of this port is much larger than that of Foochow, yet I still rank it after that city because the area commanded by it is also commanded by Canton, the southern world port, and by Nanning, the river port, and so all internal as well as indirect import and export trade must go to the other two ports. It is only the direct foreign trade that will use Yamchow. Thus, in spite of its extensive hinterland it is very improbable that it could outmatch Foochow in the future as a second-class port.

Besides the three great world ports, and the four second-class ports, I propose to construct nine third-class ports along the China coast, from north to south, as follows:

    a. Hulutao.   f. Amoy.

    b. Hoangho Port.   g. Swatow.

    c. Chefoo.   h. Tienpak.

    d. Ningpo.   i. Hoihou.

    e. Wenchow.

A. HULUTAO

Hulutao is an ice-free and deep-water port, situated on the west side of the head of Liaotung Gulf, about 60 miles from Yingkow. As a winter port for Manchuria, it is in a more advantageous position than Talien for it is about 200 miles shorter by rail to the sea than the latter and is on the edge of a rich coal field. When this coal field and the surrounding mineral resources are developed, Hulutao will become the first of the third-class ports and a good outlet for Jehol and Eastern Mongolia. This port may be projected as an alternative to Yingkow, as the sole port of Manchuria and Eastern Mongolia, if a canal could be constructed to connect it with the Liaoho. It is only by inland water communication that Yingkow could be made the important port of Manchuria in the future and it will be the same in the case of Hulutao. So if inland water communication could be secured for Hulutao it will entirely displace Yingkow. If it is found to be economically cheaper in the long run to construct a Hulutao-Liaoho Canal than to construct a deep harbor at Yingkow, the Hulutao harbor will have to be placed on the northwest side of the peninsula instead of on the southwest as at present projected. For the present site has not enough room for anchorage without building an extensive breakwater into the deep sea, which will be a very expensive work. Furthermore, there would not be room enough for city planning on the narrow peninsula, whereas on the other side, the city could be built on the mainland with unlimited space for its development.

I suggest that a sea wall be built from the northern point of Lienshanwan to the northern point of Hulutao to close up the Lienshan Bay and make it into a closed harbor, and an entrance be opened in the neck of Hulutao to the south side where deep water is found. This closed harbor will be over 10 square miles in extent but only some parts need to be dredged to the required depth at present. On the north side of the harbor, another entrance into the neighboring bay should be left open between the sea wall and the shore, and another breakwater should be built across the next bay. From there, a canal should be constructed either by cutting into the shore or by building a wall parallel with the coast line until it reaches the lowland from where a canal should be cut to connect with the Liaoho. If a canal is thus constructed for Hulutao, then it will at once take the place of Yingkow and become the first of the second-class ports.

B. THE HOANGHO PORT

The Hoangho Port will be situated at the estuary of the Hoangho on the southern side of the Gulf of Pechihli, about 80 miles from our Great Northern Port. When the Hoangho regulation is completed its estuary will be approachable by ocean steamers, and a seaport will naturally spring up there. As it commands a considerable part of the northern plain in the provinces of Shantung, Chili, and Honan and possesses the facility of inland water communication, this port is bound to become an important third-class port.

C. CHEFOO

Chefoo is an old treaty port situated on the northern

side of the Shantung Peninsula. Once it was the only ice-free port in the whole of North China. Since the development of Talien in the north and the development of Tsingtau in the south its trade has dwindled considerably. As a seaport, it will undoubtedly hold its own when the railroads in the Shantung Peninsula are developed, and the artificial harbor is completed.

D. NINGPO

Ningpo is also an old treaty port, situated on a small river, the Yungkiang, in the eastern part of Chekiang province. It has a good approach, deep water reaching right up to the estuary of the river. The harbor can be easily improved by simply training and straightening two bends along its course up to the city. Ningpo commands a very small but rich hinterland. Its people are very enterprising, and are famed for their workmanship and handicrafts second only to those of Canton. Thus Ningpo is bound to become a manufacturing city when China is industrially developed. But owing to the proximity of the Great Eastern Port, Ningpo will not likely have much import and export trade directly with foreign countries. Most of its trade will be carried on with the Great Eastern Port. So a moderate harbor for local and coast-wise traffic will be quite sufficient for Ningpo.

E. WENCHOW

Wenchow is situated near the mouth of the Wukiang in south Chekiang. This seaport has a wider hinterland than Ningpo, its surrounding districts being very productive. If railroads are developed it will undoubtedly command considerable local trade. At present the harbor is very shallow, unapproachable by even moderate-sized coastal steamers. I suggest that a new harbor at Panshiwei, north of Wenchow Island be constructed. For this purpose, a dike should be built between the northern bank and the head of Wenchow Island to block up the river entirely on the northern side of that island leaving only a lock entrance. The Wukiang should be led through the channel on the south side of the island for the purpose of reclaiming the vast expanse of the near-by shallows as well as for draining the upper stream. The approach from the southern side of Hutau Island to the port should be dredged. On the right side of the approach, a wall should be built in the shallow between Wenchow Island and Miau Island and in the shallows between Miau Island and Sanpam Island so as to form a continuous wall to prevent the silt of Wukiang from entering into the approach. Thus a permanent deep channel will be secured for the new port of Wenchow.

F. AMOY

Amoy, an old treaty port, is situated on the island of Siming. It has a great, deep, and fine harbor, commanding a considerable hinterland in southern Fukien and Kiangsi, very rich in coal and iron deposits. This port carries on a busy trade with the Malay Archipelago and the Southeastern Asian Peninsula. Most of the Chinese residents in the southern islands, Annam, Burma, Siam, and the Malay States are from the neighborhood of Amoy. So the passenger traffic between Amoy and the southern colonies is very great. If railways are developed to tap the rich iron and coal fields in the hinterland, Amoy is bound to develop into a much larger seaport than it is at present. I suggest that a modern port be constructed on the west side of the harbor to act as an outlet for the rich mineral fields of southern Fukien and Kiangsi. This port should be equipped with modern plants in order to connect land and sea transportation.

G. SWATOW

Swatow is situated at the mouth of the Hankiang at the extreme east of Kwangtung. In relation to emigration, Swatow is much similar to Amoy, for it also supplies a great number of colonists to southeastern Asia and the Malay Archipelago. So its passenger traffic with the south is just as busy as Amoy. As a seaport Swatow is far inferior to Amoy, on account of its shallow approach. But in regard to inland water communication, Swatow is in a better position as the Hankiang is navigable for many hundreds of miles inland by shallow crafts. The country around Swatow is very productive agriculturally, being second only to the Canton Delta along the Southern seaboard. In the upper reaches of the Hankiang there are very rich iron and coal deposits. The approach to the port of Swatow can be improved easily by a little training and dredging, thus making it a fine local port.

H. TIENPAK

Tienpak is situated at a point in the coast of Kwangtung province between the estuary of the West River and the island of Hainan. Its surrounding districts are rich in agricultural products and mineral deposits. So a shipping port in this part is quite necessary. Tienpak can be made into a fine harbor by entirely walling in the bay from its west side and by opening a new entrance into the deep water in the neck of the peninsula southeast of the bay. Thus a good approach could be secured. The harbor is very wide but only a part need be dredged for large vessels and the rest of the space could be used by fishing boats and other shallow crafts.

I. HOIHOU

Hoihou is situated on the north side of Hainan Island on the strait of the same name, opposite Haian on the Luichow Peninsula. Hoihou is a treaty port, similar to Amoy and Swatow, supplying a great number of colonists to the south; Hainan is a very rich but undeveloped island. Only the land along the coast is cultivated, the central part being still covered by thick forests and inhabited by aborigines, and it is very rich in mineral deposits. When the whole island is fully developed, the port of Hoihou will be a busy harbor for export and import traffic. The harbor of Hoihou is very shallow, and so even small vessels have to anchor miles away in the roadstead outside. This is very inconvenient for passengers and cargoes, so the improvement of the Hoihou harbor is a necessity. Furthermore this harbor will be the ferry point between this island and the mainland for railway traffic when the railway systems of the mainland and the island are completed.

FISHING HARBORS

As regards fishing harbors all our first-, second-, and third-class ports must also furnish facilities and accommodations for fishery. Thus all of these, i.e., three first-class ports, four second-class ports, and nine third-class ports, will be fishing harbors as well. But besides these sixteen ports there is still room and need to construct more fishing harbors along the coast of China. I propose, therefore, that five fishing harbors be constructed along the northern coast, that is, along the coast of Fengtien, Chihli, and Shantung, as follows:

(1) Antung, on Yalu River, on the border of Korea.

(2) Haiyangtao, on the Yalu Bay, south of Liaotung Peninsula.

(3) Chinwangtao, on the coast of Chihli, between the Liaotung and Pechihli gulfs, the present ice-free port of Chihli province.

(4) Lungkau, on the northwestern side of Shantung Peninsula.

(5) Shitauwan, at the southeastern point of the Shantung Peninsula.

Six fishing harbors should be constructed along the eastern coast, that is, along the coasts of Kiangsu, Chekiang, and Fukien, as follows:

(6) Shinyangkang, on the eastern coast of Kiangsu, south of the old mouth of the Hoangho.

(7) Luszekang, at the northern point of the Yangtze Estuary.

(8) Changtukang, in the midst of Chusan Archipelago.

(9) Shipu, north of Sammen Bay, east of Chekiang.

(10) Funing, between Foochow and Wenchow, east of Fukien.

(11) Meichow Harbor, north of Meichow Island, between Foochow and Amoy.

Four fishing harbors should be constructed on the southern coast, that is, along the seaboard of Kwangtung and Hainan Island, as follows.

(12) Sanmei, on the eastern coast of Kwangtung, between Hongkong and Swatow.

(13) Sikiang Mouth. This harbor should be on the northern side of Wangkum Island. When the Sikiang Mouth is regulated, the Wangkum Island will be connected with the mainland by a sea wall, so a good harbor site could thus be provided.

(14) Haian, situated at the end of the Luichow Peninsula opposite to Hoihou, on the other side of Hainan Strait.

(15) Yulinkang, a fine natural harbor at the extreme south of the Hainan Island.

These fifteen fishing harbors with the greater ports, numbering 31 in all, will link up the whole coast line of China from Antung, on the Korean border to Yamchow, near the Annam border, providing, on an average, a port for every 100 miles of coast line. This completes my project of seaports and fishing harbors for China.

At first sight objections migh be raised that too many seaports and fishing harbors are provided for one country. But I must remind my readers that this one country, China, is as big as Europe and has a population larger than that of Europe. If we take a similar length of the coast line of western Europe we would see that there are many more ports in Europe than in China. Besides, the coast line of Europe is many times longer than that of China, and in every hundred miles of the European coast line there are more than one considerable sized port. Take Holland, for instance. Its whole area is not larger than the hinterland of Swatow, one of our third-class seaports, yet it possesses two first-class ports, Amsterdam and Rotterdam, and numerous small fishing ports. Let us also compare our country with the United States of America in regard to seaports. America has only one fourth the population of China yet the number of ports on her Atlantic coast alone is many times more than the number provided in my plan. Thus, this number of ports for China for the future is but a bare necessity. And I have considered only those that will pay from the beginning so as to adhere strictly to the principle of remuneration that was laid down at the outset of my first program. See Map XVI.

PART V

THE ESTABLISHMENT OF SHIPBUILDING YARDS

When China is well developed according to my programs, the possession of an oversea mercantile fleet, of ships for coastal and inland water transportation, and of a large fishing fleet will be an urgent necessity. Before the outbreak of the late World War, the world's seagoing tonnage was 45,000,000 tons. If China is equally developed industrially, according to the proportion of her population, she would need at least 10,000,000 tons of oversea and coastal shipping for her transportation service. The building of this tonnage must be a part of our industrial development scheme; for cheap materials and labor can be obtained in the country, and so we could build ships for ourselves much cheaper than any foreign country could do for us. And besides the building of a seagoing fleet, we have to build our inland water crafts and fishing fleets. Foreign shipping yards could not do this service for us on account of the impracticability of transporting such numerous small crafts across the ocean. Thus, in any case, China has to put up her own yards to build her inland water crafts and fishing fleets. So the establishment of ship building yards is a necessary as well as a profitable undertaking from the beginning. The shipping yards should be established at such river and coastal ports that have the facility of supplying materials and labor. All the yards should be under one central management. Large capital should be invested in the project so as to procure a yearly output of 2,000,000 tons of various kinds of vessels.

All types of vessels should be standardized both in design and equipment. The old and wasteful types of inland water crafts and fishing boats should be replaced by modern efficient designs. The inland water crafts should be designed on the basis of certain standard draughts such as the 2-foot, 5-foot, and 10-foot classes. The fishing trawlers should be standardized into the one-day, the five-day, and the ten-day service class. The coastal transports should be standardized into the 2,000-, the 4,000-, and the 6,000-ton class, and for oversea transports we should have standardized ships of 12,000-, 24,000-, and 36,000-ton classes. Thus, the many thousands of inland water crafts and fishing junks that now ply the rivers, lakes, and coasts of China may be displaced by new and cheaper crafts of a few standard types which could perform better services at less expense.

PROGRAM IV

In my first and third programs, I have described my plans for the Northwestern Railway System and the Southwestern Railway System. The former is for the purpose of relieving the congestion of population in the coast districts and the Yangtze Valley by opening up for colonization the vast unpopulated territory in Mongolia and Sinkiang, as well as of developing the Great Northern Port. The latter is for the purpose of exploiting the mineral resources of Southwestern China, as well as of developing the Great Southern Port—Canton. More railroads will be needed for the adequate development of the whole country. So in this fourth program, I shall deal entirely with railroads which will complete the 100,000 miles proposed in my introductory part of this International Development Scheme. The program will be as follows:

I. The Central Railway System.

II. The Southeastern Railway System.

III. The Northeastern Railway System.

IV. The Extension of the Northwestern Railway System.

V. The Highland Railway System.

VI. The Establishment of Locomotive and Car Factories.

PART I

The Central Railway System

This will be the most important railway system in China. The area which it serves comprises all of China

Proper north of the Yangtze and a part of Mongolia and Sinkiang. The economic nature of this vast region is that the southeastern part is densely populated while the northwestern part is thinly populated, and that the southeastern part possesses great mineral wealth while the northwestern part possesses great potential agricultural resources. So every line of this system will surely pay as the Peking-Mukden line has proved.

With the Great Eastern Port and the Great Northern Port as termini of this system of railroads, I propose that, besides the existing and projected lines in this region, the following be constructed, all of which shall constitute the Central Railway System.

    a. The Great Eastern Port-Tarbogotai line.
    b. The Greatern Port-Urga line.
    c. The Great Eastern Port-Uliassutai line.
    d. The Nanking-Loyang line.
    e. The Nanking-Hankow line.
    f. The Sian-Tatung line.
    g. The Sian-Ninghsia line.
    h. The Sian-Hankow line.
    i. The Sian-Chungking line.
    j. The Lanchow-Chungking line.
    k. The Ansichow-Iden line.
    l. The Chochiang-Koria line.
    m. The Great Northern Port-Hami line.
    n. The Great Northern Port-Sian line.
    o. The Great Northern Port-Hankow line.

p. The Hoangho Port-Hankow line.
q. The Chefoo-Hankow line.
r. The Haichow-Tsinan line.
s. The Haichow-Hankow line.
t. The Haichow-Nanking line.
u. The Sinyangkang-Hankow line.
v. The Luszekang-Nanking line.
w. The Coast line.
x. The Hwoshan-Kashing line.

A. THE GREAT EASTERN PORT-TARBOGOTAI LINE

This line begins at the Great Eastern Port on the seaboard, and runs in a northwesterly direction to Tarbogotai on the Russian frontier, covering a distance of about 3,000 miles. If Shanghai be the Great Eastern Port, the Shanghai-Nanking Railway will form its first section. But if Chapu be chosen, then this line should skirt the Taihu Lake on the southwest through the cities of Huchow, Changhing, and Liyang to Nanking, then crossing the Yangtze at a point south of Nanking, to Chiantsiao and Tingyuen. Thence, the line turns westward to Showchow and Yingshang, and enters Honan province at Sintsai. After crossing the Peking-Hankow line at Kioshan and passing Piyang, Tanghsien, and Tengchow, it turns northwestward to Sichwan and Kingtsekwan, and enters the province of Shensi. Ascending the Tan Kiang Valley, it passes through Lungkucha and Shangchow, and crosses the Tsinling Pass to Lantien and Sian, the capital of Shensi, formerly the capital of China. From Sian, it goes westward, following the valley of the Weiho. It passes through Chowchih, Meihsien, and Paoki and enters the province of Kansu at

Sancha, thence proceeding to Tsinchow, Kungchang, Titao, and Lanchow, the capital of Kansu. From Lanchow it follows the old highway which leads into Liangchow, Kanchow, Suchow, Yumen, and Ansichow. Thence it crosses the desert in a northwesterly direction to Hami, where it turns westward to Turfan. At Turfan this line meets the Northwestern Railway System and runs on the latter's track to Urumochi and Manass where it leaves that track and proceeds northwesterly to Tarbogotai on the frontier, crossing the Shair Mountain on the way. This line runs from one end of the country to the other encountering in its entire length of 3,000 miles only four mountain passes, all of which are not impassable for they have been used from time immemorial, as trade highways of Asia.

B. THE GREAT EASTERN PORT-URGA LINE

The line starts from the Great Eastern Port and uses the same track as line (a) as far as Tingyuen, the second city after crossing the Yangtze River at Nanking. From Tingyuen, its own track begins and the line proceeds in a northwesterly direction to Hwaiyuan, on the Hwai River, thence to Mongcheng, Kwoyang, and Pochow. Turning more northward, it crosses the Anhwei border into Honan, and passing through Kweiteh it crosses the Honan border into Shantung. After passing through Tsaohsien, Tingtao, and Tsaochow, it crosses the Hoangho and enters Chihli province. Passing through Kaichow it re-enters Honan to Changteh, thence it follows the Tsingchangho valley, in a northwesterly direction, across the Honan border into Shansi. Here the line enters the northern corner of the vast iron and coal field of Shansi. After entering Shansi, the line follows the river valley to Liaochow and Yicheng, and crosses the watershed into the Tungkwoshui Valley to

DEVELOPMENT OF CHINA   119

Yutse and Taiyuan. From Taiyuan, it proceeds northwestward through another rich iron and coal field of Shansi to Kolan. Thence, it turns westward to Poate, where it crosses the Hoangho to Fuku, in the northeastern corner of Shensi. From Fuku, the line proceeds northward, cuts through the Great Wall into the Suiyuan District and crosses the Hoangho to Saratsi. Fro mSaratsi, the line runs in a northwesterly direction across the vast prairie to Junction A of the Northwestern Trunk Line, where it joins the common track of the Dolon Nor-Urga line to Urga. This line runs from a thickly populated country at one end in Central China to the vast thinly populated but fertile regions of Central Mongolia, having a distance of about 1,300 miles from Tingyuen to Junction A.

C. THE GREAT EASTERN PORT-ULIASSUTAI LINE

Starting from the Great Eastern Port, this line follows line (a) as far as Tingyuen, and line (b) as far as Pochow. At Pochow, it branches off on its own track and proceeds westward across the border to Luye, in Honan. Thence it turns northwestward to Taikang, Tungsu, and Chungmow where it meets the Hailan line and runs in the same direction with it to Chengchow, Jungyang, and Szeshui. From Szeshui it crosses the Hoangho to Wenhsien, thence to Hwaiking and over the Honan border into Shansi, It now passes through Yangcheng, Chinshui, and Fowshan to Pingyang where it crosses the Fen River and proceeds to Puhsien and Taning, then westward to the border where it crosses the Hoangho into Shensi. Thence it proceeds to Yenchang, and follows the Yenshui Valley to Yenan, Siaokwan, and Tsingpien. Then running along the south side of the Great Wall, it enters Kansu, and crosses the Hoangho to Ninghsia. From Ninghsia, it proceeds northwestward across the

Alashan Mountain to Tingyuanying at the edge of the desert. Thence it proceeds in a straight line northwestward to Junction B of the Northwestern Railway System, where it joins that system and runs to Uliassutai. This part of the line passes through desert and grassland both of which could be improved by irrigation. The distance of this line from Pochow to Junction B is 1,800 miles.

D. THE NANKING-LOYANG LINE

This line runs between two former capitals of China, passes through a very populous and fertile country, and taps a very rich coal field at the Loyang end. It starts from Nanking, running on the common track of lines (a) and (b) and branches off at Hwaiyuan westward to Taiho. After passing Taiho, it crosses the Anhwei border into Honan. Thence it runs alongside the left bank of the Tashaho to Chowkiakow, a large commercial town. From Chowkiakow, it proceeds to Linying where it crosses the Peking-Hankow line thence to Hiangcheng and Yuchow where the rich coal field of Honan lies. After Yuchow it crosses the Sungshan watershed to Loyang where it meets the Hailan line running from east to west. This line is about 300 miles from Hwaiyuan to Loyang.

E. THE NANKING-HANKOW LINE

This line will run alongside the left bank of the Yangtzekiang, connecting with Kiukiang by a branch line. It starts on the opposite side of Nanking and goes southwest to Hochow, Wuweichow and Anking, the capital of Anhwei province. After Anking, it continues in the same direction to Susung and Hwangmei, where a branch should be projected to Siaochikow, thence across the Yangtze River to

Kiukiang. After Hwangmei, the line turns westward to Kwangchi, then northwestward to Kishui, and finally westward to Hankow. It covers a distance of about 350 miles through a comparatively level country.

F. THE SIAN-TATUNG LINE

This line starts from Sian and runs northward to Sanyuan, Yaochow, Tungkwan, Yichun, Chungpu, Foochow, Kanchuan, and Yenan, where it meets the Great Eastern Port-Uliassutai line. From Yenan, it turns northeastward to Suiteh, Michih, and Kiachow on the right bank of the Hoangho. Thence it runs along the same bank to the junction of the Weifen River with the Hoangho (on the opposite side), where it crosses the Hoangho to the Weifen Valley and proceeds to Singhsien and Kolan, there crossing the Great Eastern Port-Urga line. From Kolan it proceeds to Wuchai and Yangfang, where it crosses the Great Wall to Sochow and then Tatung there meeting the Peking-Suiyuan line. This line is about 600 miles long. It passes through the famous oil field in Shensi, and the northern border of the northwestern Shansi coal field. At Tatung, where it ends, it joins the Peking-Suiyuan line and through the section from Tatung to Kalgan it will connect with the future Northwestern System which will link Kalgan and Dolon Nor together.

G. THE SIAN-NINGHSIA LINE

This line will start from Sian in a northwesterly direction to Kingyanghsien, Shunhwa, and Sanshui. After Sanshui, it crosses the Shensi border into Kansu at Chengning and then turns west to Ningchow. From Ningchow, it follows the Hwan Valley along the left bank of the river up to Kingyangfu and Hwanhsien, where it leaves the bank and proceeds to Tsingping and Pingyuan, where it meets the Hwan River again and follows that valley up to the watershed. After crossing the watershed, it proceeds to Lingchow, then across the Hoangho to Ninghsia. This line covers a distance of about 400 miles and passes through a rich mineral and petroleum country.

H. THE SIAN-HANKOW LINE

This is a very important line connecting the richest portion of the Hoangho Valley with the richest portion of the central section of the Yangtze Valley. It starts from Sian on the track of line (a), crosses the Tsingling and descends the Tankiang Valley as far as Sichwan. At this point, it branches off southward across the border into Hupeh, and following the left bank of the Han River, passes Laohokow to Fencheng, opposite Siangyang. After Fencheng, it follows continuously the same bank of the Han River to Anlu, thence proceeding in a direct line southeastward to Hanchwan and Hankow. This line is about 300 miles long.

I. THE SIAN-CHUNGKING LINE

This line starts from Sian almost directly southward, crosses the Tsingling Mountain into the Han Valley, passes through Ningshen, Shihchuan, and Tzeyang, ascends the Jenho Valley across the southern border of Shensi into the province of Sbechwan at Tachuho. Then crossing the watershed of the Tapashan into the Tapingho Valley, it follows that valley down to Suiting and Chuhsien. Thence it turns to the left side of the valley to Linshui and follows the trade road to Kiangpeh and Chungking. The entire distance of this line is about 450 miles through a very productive region and rich timber land.

J. THE LANCHOW-CHUNGKING LINE

This line starts from Lanchow southwestward and follows the same route as line (a) as far as Titao. Thence, it branches off and ascends the Taoho Valley across the Minshan watershed into the Heishui Valley following it down to Kiaichow and Pikow. After Pikow, it crosses the Kansu border into Szechwan and proceeds to Chaohwa, where the Heishuiho joins the Kialing. From Chaohwa, it follows the course of the Kialing River down to Paoning, Shunking, Hochow, and Chungking. The line is about 600 miles long, running through a very productive and rich mineral land.

K. THE ANSICHOW-IDEN LINE

This line passes through the fertile belt of land between the Gobi Desert and the Altyntagh Mountain. Although this strip of land is well watered by numerous mountain streams yet it is very sparsely populated, owing to the lack of means of communication. When this line is completed, this strip of land will be most valuable to Chinese colonists. The line starts from Ansichow westward to Tunhwang, and skirts the southern edge of the Lobnor Swamp to Chochiang. From Chochiang, it proceeds in the same direction via Cherchen to Iden where it connects with the terminus of the Northwestern System. With this System, it forms a continuous and direct line from the Great Eastern Port to Kashgar at the extreme west end of China. This line from Ansichow to Iden is about 800 miles in length.

L. THE CHOCHIANG-KORIA LINE

This line runs across the desert alongside the lower part of the Tarim River. The land on both sides of the line is well watered and will be valuable for colonization as soon as the railroad is completed. This line is about 250 miles in length and connects with the line that runs along the northern edge of the desert. It is a short cut between fertile lands on the two sides of the desert.

M. THE GREAT NORTHERN PORT-HAMI LINE

This line runs from the Great Northern Port in a northwesterly direction by way of Paoti and Siangho to Peking. From Peking it runs on the same track with the Peking-Kalgan Railway to Kalgan, where it ascends the Mongolian Plateau. Then it follows the caravan road northwestward to Chintai, Bolutai, Sessy, and Tolibulyk. From Tolibulyk, it takes a straight line westward crossing the prairie and desert of both the Inner and Outer Mongolia to Hami where it connects with the Great Eastern Port-Tarbogotai line which runs almost directly west to Urumochi, the capital of Sinkiang. Thus, it will be the direct line from Urumochi to Peking and the Great Northern Port. This line is about 1,500 miles in length, the greater part of which will run through arable land and so when it is completed it will form one of the most valuable railways for colonization.

N. THE GREAT NORTHERN PORT-SIAN LINE

This line will run westward from the Great Northern Port to Tientsin. From here it runs southwestward to Hokien, passing through Tsinghai and Tachen. From Hokien, it runs more westerly to Shentseh, Wuki, and Chengting where it joins the Chengtai line as well as crosses the Kinhan line. From Chengting it takes the same road as the narrow gauge Chengtai line which has to be reconstructed into standard gauge so as to facilitate through trains to Taiyuan and farther on. From Taiyuan it runs southwestward to Kiaocheng, Wenshui, Fenchow, Sichow, and Taning. After Taning it turns westward and crossing the Hoangho, it turns southwestward to Yichwan, Lochwan, and Chungpu where it joins the Sian-Tatung line and runs on the same tracks to Sian. Its length is about 700 miles over very rich and extensive iron, coal, and petroleum fields, as well as productive agricultural lands.

O. THE GREAT NORTHERN PORT-HANKOW LINE

This line starts from the Great Northern Port skirting the coast to Petang, Taku, and Chikow, thence to Yenshan and crosses the Chili border into Shantung at Loling. From Loling, it goes to Tehping, Linyi and Yucheng where it crosses the Tiestsin-Pukow line, proceeds tor Tungchang and Fanhsien, and then crosses the Hoangho to Tsaochow. After Tsaochow it passes the Shantung border into Honan, crossing the Hailan line to Suichow. From Suichow it proceeds to Taikang where it crosses line (c), then to Chenchow and Chowkiakow where it crosses line (d) and thence to Siangcheng, Sintsai, Kwangchow, and Kwangshan. After Kwangshan it crosses the boundary mountain into Hupeh, passing through Hwangan to Hankow. This line is about 700 miles long, running from the Great Northern Port to the commercial center of central China.

P. THE HOANGHO PORT-HANKOW LINE

This line starts from the Hoangho Port in a southwesterly direction to Pohsing, Sincheng, and Changshan, then across the Kiauchow-Tsinan line to Poshan. Thence it ascends the watershed into the Wen Valley to Taian where it crosses the Tientsin-Pukow line to Ningyang and Tsining. From Tsining it proceeds in a straight line southwestward to Pochow in Anhwei, and Sintsai in Honan. At Sintsai it joins the Great Northern Port-Hankow line to Hankow. The distance of this line from the Hoangho Port to Sintsai is about 400 miles.

Q. THE CHEFOO-HANKOW LINE

This line starts at Chefoo of the northern side of the Shantung Peninsula and crosses that Peninsula to Tsimo, on the southern side, via Laiyang and Kinkiakow. From Tsimo it proceeds southwestward across the shallow mud flat at the head of Kiauchow Bay in a straight line to Chucheng. After Chucheng it crosses the watershed into the Shuho Valley toChuchow and Ichow, then proceeds to Hsuchow where it meets the Tientsin-Pukow line and the Hailan line. From Hsuchow it runs on the same track with the Tientsin-Pukow line as far as Suchow in Anhwei, then branches off to Mongcheng and Yinchow, and crosses the border into Honan at Kwangchow, where it meets the Great Northern Port-Hankow line and proceeds together to Hankow. This line from Chefoo to Kwangchow is about 550 miles in length.

R. THE HAICHOW-TSINAN LINE

This line starts from Haichow following the Linhung River to Kwantunpu, then turns westward to Ichow. From Ichow it turns first northward then northwestward, passing by Mongyin and Sintai to Tai-an. At Tai-an it joins the Tsinpu line and proceeds in the same track to Tsinan. This line covers a distance, from Haichow to Tai-an, of about 110 miles, tapping the coal and iron fields of southern Shantung.

S. THE HAICHOW-HANKOW LINE

This line starts at Haichow in a southwesterly direction,

DEVELOPMENT OF CHINA 127

goes to Shuyang and Sutsien, probably in the same route as the projected Hailan line. From Sutsien it proceeds to Szechow and Hwaiyuan, where it crosses the Great Eastern Port Urga and Uliassutai lines. After Hwaiyuan it goes to Showchow and Chenyangkwan, thence continuing in the same direction across the southeastern corner of Honan and the boundary mountain into Hupeh, proceeds to Macheng and Hankow, covering a distance of about 400 miles.

T. THE HAICHOW-NANKING LINE

This line goes from Haichow southward to Antung then inclining a little south to Hwaian. After Hwaian it crosses the Paoying Lake (which will be reclaimed according to the regulation of the Hwaiho in Part IV, Program II) to Tienchang and Luho, thence to Nanking. Distance, about 180 miles.

U. THE SINYANGKANG-HANKOW LINE

This line starts from Sinyangkang to Yencheng, then crossing the Tasung Lake (which will be reclaimed) to Hwaian. From Hwaian it turns southwestward passing over the southeastern corner of the Hungtse Lake (which will also be reclaimed) to Suyi, in Anhwei. After Suyi, it crosses the Tientsin-Pukow line near Mingkwang, to Tingyuen, where it meets lines (b) and (c). After Tingyuen, it proceeds to Lu-an and Hwoshan, then crosses the boundary mountain into Hupeh passing through Lotien to Hankow, a distance of about 420 miles.

V. THE LUSZEKANG-NANKING LINE

This line starts at Luszekang, a fishing harbor to be constructed at the extremity of the northern point of the Yangtze Estuary. From Luszekang it proceeds westward to Tungchow where it turns northwestward to Jukao, and then westward to Taichow, Yangchow, Luho, and Nanking. This line is about 200 miles long.

W. THE COAST LINE

This line starts at the Great Northern Port, and follows the Great Northern Port-Hankow line as far as Chikow, where it begins its own line. Keeping along the coast, it crosses the Chili border to the Hoangho Port, in Shantung, then proceeds to Laichow where it takes a straight cut away from the coast to Chaoyuan and Chefoo, thus avoiding the projected Chefoo-Weihsien line. From Chefoo it proceeds southeastward through Ninghai to Wenteng, where one branch runs to Jungcheng and another to Shihtao. The main line turns southwestward to Haiyang and Kinkiakow, where it joins the Chefoo-Hankow line, and follows it as far as the western side of Kiauchow Bay, thence southward to Lingshanwei. From Lingshanwei the line proceeds southwestward along the coast to Jichao, and crosses the Shantung border into Kiangsu, passing Kanyu to Haichow. Thence it proceeds southeastward to Yencheng, Tungtai. Tungchow, Haimen, and Tsungming Island which will be connected with the mainland by the regulation works of Yangtze embankment. From Tsungming trains can be ferried over to Shanghai. This line from Chikow to Tsungming is about 1,000 miles in length.

X. THE HWOSHAN-WUHU-SOOCHOW-KASHING LINE

This line starts from Hwoshan to Shucheng and Wuwei, then across the Yangtze River to Wuhu. After Wuhu it goes to Kaoshun, Liyang, and Ihing, then crosses over the northern end of Taihu (which will be reclaimed) to Soochow, where it meets the Shanghai-Nanking line. From

Soochow it turns southward to Kashing on the Shanghai-Hangchow line. This line runs over very populous and rich districts of Anhwei and Kiangsu provinces, covering a distance of about 300 miles, which will form the greater part of the shortest line from Shanghai to Hankow.

PART II

THE SOUTHEASTERN RAILWAY SYSTEM

This system covers the irregular triangle which is formed by the Coast line between the Great Eastern and the Great Southern Ports, as the base, by the Yangtze River from Chungking to Shanghai, as one side, and by line (a) of the Canton-Chungking Railway as the other side, with Chungking as the apex. This triangle comprises the provinces of Chekiang, Fukien, and Kiangsi, and a part respectively of Kiangsu, Anhwei, Hupeh, Hunan, and Kwangtung. This region is very rich in mineral and agricultural products, especially iron and coal deposits whch are found everywhere. And the whole region is thickly populated. So railway construction will be very remunerative.

With the Great Eastern Port and the Great Southern Port and the second- and third-class ports that lie between the two as termini of this system of railroads, I propose that the following lines be constructed:

  a. The Great Eastern Port-Chungking Line.
  b. The Great Eastern Port-Canton Line.
  c. The Foochow-Chinkiang Line.
  d. The Foochow-Wuchang Line.
  e. The Foochow-Kweilin Line.
  f. The Wenchow-Shenchow Line.

g. The Amoy-Kienchang Line.
h. The Amoy-Canton Line.
i. The Swatow-Changteh Line.
j. The Nanking-Siuchow Line.
k. The Nanking-Kaying Line.
l. The Coast Line between the Great Eastern and Great Southern Ports.
m. The Kienchang-Yuanchow Line.

A. THE GREAT EASTERN PORT-CHUNGKING LINE

This line connects the commercial center of western China—Chungking—with the Great Eastern Port in almost a straight route south of the Yangtze River. It starts from the Great Eastern Port and goes to Hangchow, then through Linan, Ghanghwa, to Hweichow, in Anhwei. From Hweichow it proceeds to Siuning and Kimen, then crosses the border into Kiangsi and passing Hukow reaches Kiukiang. From Kiukiang it follows the right bank of the Yangtze, crosses the Hupeh border to Hingkwochow and then proceeds to Tungshan and Tsungyang, where it passes over the border to Yochow in Hunan. From Yochow it takes a straight line across the Tungting Lake (which will be reclaimed) to Changteh. From Changteh it proceeds up the Liu Shui Valley, passing through Tzeli, and crossing the Hunan border to Hofeng, in Hupeh and then to Shinan and Lichwan. At Shinan a branch should be projected northeastward to Ichang, and at Lichwan another branch should be projected northwestward to Wanhsien, both on the left side of the Yangtze River. After Lichwan it crosses the Hupeh border into Szechwan, passing Shihchu to Foochow, then passes the Wukiang and proceeds along the

DEVELOPMENT OF CHINA 131

right side of the Yangtze River as far as lines (a) and (b) of the Canton-Chungking Railway and then crosses together on the same bridge to Chungking on the other side of the river. The length of this line including branches, is about 1,200 miles.

B. THE GREAT EASTERN PORT-CANTON LINE

This is a straight line from one first-class seaport to another. It starts from the Great Eastern Port and goes to Hangchow, then turning southwestward, follows the left bank of the Tsien Tang River through Fuyang, Tunglu to Yenchow and Chuchow. Then it proceeds across the Chekiang-Kiangsi border to Kwangsin. From Kwangsin it goes through Shangtsing and Kinki to Kienchang, then proceeds to Nanfeng, Kwangchang, and Ningtu. After Ningtu it proceeds to Yutu, Sinfeng, Lungnan, and crossing the boundary mountain of Kiangsi and Kwangtung, to Changning. Thence via Tsungfa it goes to Canton, covering a distance of about 900 miles.

C. THE FOOCHOW-CHINKIANG LINE

This line starts from Foochow, goes by way of Loyuan and Ningteh to Fuan, and then proceeds across the Fukien-Chekiang border to Taishun, Kingning, Yunho, and Chuchow. Thence it proceeds to Wuyi, Yiwu, Chukih, and Hangchow. After Hangchow it goes to Tehtsing and Huchow and then crosses the Chekiang border into Kiangsu. Then it proceeds by way of Ihing, Kintan, and Tanyang to Chinkiang. This line is about 550 miles in length.

D. THE FOOCHOW-WUCHANG LINE

This line starts from Foochow and following the left bank of the Min River and passing Shuikow and Yenping reaches Shaowu. After Shaowu, it proceeds across the Fukien border into Kiangsi and then passes through Kienchang and Fuchow to Nanchang, the capital of Kiangsi. From Nanchang it proceeds to Hingkwo, in Hupeh, and passes on to Wuchang, the capital of Hupeh. It covers a distance of about 550 miles.

E. THE FOOCHOW-KWEILIN LINE

This line starts from Foochow, crosses the Min River and proceeds by way of Yungfu, Tatien, Ningyang, and Liencheng to Tingchow. Thence it crosses the Fukien-Kiangsi border to Shuikin. From Shuikin it proceeds to Yutu and Kanchow and then to Shangyiu and Chungyi. After Chungyi it crosses the Kiangsi-Hunan border to Kweiyanghsien and Chenchow, where it crosses the Canton-Hankow line to Kweiyangchow. Thence it continues to Sintien, Ningyuan, and Taochow, where it meets lines (a) and (b) of the Canton-Chungking Railway. After Taochow it turns southward following the Taoho Valley to the Kwangsi border and then crossing it, proceeds to Kweilin. This line covers a distance of about 750 miles.

F. THE WENCHOW-SHENCHOW LINE

This line begins from the new Wenchow Port and follows the left bank of the Wukiang as far as Tsingtien. From Tsingtien it proceeds to Chuchow and Suenping and turns westward across the Chekiang border to Yushan in Kiangsi. After Yushan it goes to Tehsing, Loping, and then skirting the southern shore of Poyang Lake goes through Yukan to Nanchang, the capital of Kiangsi. From Nanchang it proceeds to Juichow, Shangkao, and Wantsai, then crosses the Kiangsi border to Liuyang in Hunan, and Changsha, the capital of Hunan. After Changsha it goes to Ningsiang, Anhwa, and Shenchow where it connects with line (a) of the Canton-Chungking Railway, and with the Shasi-Singyi line. This line covers a distance of about 850 miles.

G. THE AMOY-KIENCHANG LINE

This line starts from the new port of Amoy and goes to Changtai, then following the Kiulungkiang to Changping, Ningyang, Tsingliu, and Kienning. After Kienning it proceeds across the Kiangsi border to Kienchang, where it connects with the Great Eastern Port-Canton line, the Foochow-Wuchang line, and the Kienchang-Yuanchow line. This line covers a distance of about 250 miles.

H. THE AMOY-CANTON LINE

This line starts at the new port of Amoy, and proceeds to Changchow, Nantsing, and Siayang, where it crosses the Fukien border to Tapu, in Kwangtung. From Tapu it goes to Tsungkow, Kaying, Hinning, and Wuhwa. After Wuhwa it crosses the watershed between the Hankiang and the Tungkiang rivers to Lungchan, then following the Tungkiang down to Hoyun, it crosses another watershed to Lungmoon, Tsengshin and Canton. This line covers a distance of about 400 miles.

I. THE SWATOW-CHANGTEH LINE

This line starts from Swatow, proceeds to Chaochow, Kaying, and then crosses the Kwangtung border to Changning in Kiangsi. From Changning it crosses the watershed into Kungkiang Valley and follows that river down to Hweichang and Kanchow. From Kanchow it proceeds to Lungchuan, Yungning, and Lienhwa, where it crosses the Kiangsi border into Hunan. After that, it proceeds to Chuchow and Changsha, the capital of Hunan. From Changsha it goes to Ningsiang, Yiyang, and Changteh where it ends, connecting with the Great Eastern Port-Chungking line, and the Shasia-Singyi line. This line covers a distance of about 650 miles.

J. THE NANKING-SIUCHOW LINE

This line starts from Nanking and runs along the right bank of the Yangtze to Taiping, Wuhu, Tungling, Chichow, and Tungliu. After Tungliu it passes over the Anhwei border into Kiangsi, at Pengtseh, and goes to Hukow. At Hukow it meets the Great Eastern Port-Chungking line and crosses the bridge together with that line to the projected Poyang Port. From the Poyang Port it runs along the west shore of the Poyang Lake through Nanking and Wucheng to Nanchang, where it meets the Wenchow-Shenchow and Foochow-Wuchang lines. From Nanchang it proceeds up the Kan Kiang Valley, via Linkiang to Kian, where it crosses the projected Kienchang-Yuanchow line. After Kian, it proceeds to Kanchow where it crosses the Foochow-Kweilin line. Thence it goes to Nankanghsien and Nanan. After Nanan it crosses the boundary mountain, Tayuling, into Kwangtung at Nanyung, thence passes through Chihing to Siuchow, where it meets the Canton-Hankow line. This line covers a distance of about 800 miles.

K. THE NANKING-KAYING LINE

This line starts from Nanking, proceeds to Lishui and Kaoshun and then crosses the Kiangsu border into Anhwei at Suencheng. From Suencheng it proceeds to Ningkwo and Hweichow. After Hweichow it crosses the Anhwei border into Chekiang, passing through Kaihwa, Changshan, and Kiangshan, and leaving Chekiang enters Fukien at

Pucheng. From Pucheng it proceeds via Kienningfu to Yenping where it crosses the Foochow-Wuchang line and then goes through Shahsien and Yungan to Ningyang, where it meets the Foochow-Kweilin and Amoy-Kienchang lines. From Ningyang it proceeds to Lungyen and Yungting, then joining the Amoy-Canton line at Tsungkow proceeds together to Kaying, its terminus. This line runs over a distance of about 750 miles.

L. THE COAST LINE BETWEEN THE GREAT EASTERN AND THE GREAT SOUTHERN PORTS

This line starts from the Great Southern Port—Canton—proceeds in the same direction as the Canton-Kowloon line as far as Shelung and then goes its own way following the course of the Tungkiang River to Waichow. From Waichow it proceeds to Samtochuck, Haifung, and Lukfung, then turning northeastward goes to Kityang and Chaochow. After Chaochow it goes to Jaoping, then crossing the Kwangtung-Fukien border to Chaoan. Thence it proceeds to Yunsiao, Changpu, Changchow, and Amoy. From Amoy it proceeds to Chuanchow, Hinghwa, and Foochow, the capital of Fukien. After Foochow it proceeds in the same direction as the Foochow-Chinkiang line, as far as Fuan, then turns eastward to Funing, and northward to Futing. After Futing it crosses the Fukien border into Chekiang and proceeds through Pingyang to Wenchow. At Wenchow it crosses the Wukiang and proceeds to Lotsing, Hwangyen, and Taichow. Thence, it proceeds through Ninghai to Ningpo, its own terminus, where it connects with the Ningpo-Hangchow line, thus linking it up with the Great Eastern Port via Hangchow. This line covers a distance from Canton to Ningpo of about 1,100 miles,

M. THE KIENCHANG-YUANCHOW LINE

This line starts from Kienchang and runs through Yihwang, Loan, Yungfeng, and Kishui to Kian, where it crosses the Nanking-Siuchow line. After Kian it proceeds to Yungsin and Lienhwa where it meets the Swatow-Changteh line. Thence it crosses the Kiangsi border into Hunan, at Chaling, then through Anjen to Hengchow where it crosses the Canton-Hankow line. From Hengchow the line proceeds to Paoking where it crosses line (a) of the Canton-Chungking Railway then westward to Yuanchow, its terminus, where it joins with the Shasi-Singyi line. This line covers a distance of about 550 miles. The total length of this Southeastern Railway System is about 9,000 miles.

PART III

THE NORTHEASTERN RAILWAY SYSTEM

This system will cover the whole of Manchuria, a part of Mongolia, and a part of Chihli province—an area of nearly 500,000 square miles, with a population of 25,000,000. This region is surrounded by mountains on three sides and opens on the south to the Liaotung Gulf. Amidst these three mountain ranges lies a vast and fertile plain drained by three rivers—the Nonni on the north, the Sungari on the northeast, and the Liaoho on the south. This part of China was once regarded as a desert, but since the completion of the Chinese Eastern Railway it has been found to be the most productive soil in China. It supplies the whole of Japan and a part of China with nitrogenous food in the form of soya bean. This bean, the wonderful properties of which were early discovered by the Chinese, contains the richest nitrogenous substance among vegetables and has been used as a meat substitute for many thousand years.

Vegetable milk is extracted from this bean, and from this milk various kinds of preparations are made. The extraction from this bean has been proved by modern chemists to be richer than any kind of meat. The Chinese and the Japanese have used this kind of artificial meat and milk from time immemorial. Recently food administrators in Europe and America have paid great attention to this meat substitute, while the export of soya bean to Europe and America has steadily increased. This Manchu-Mongolian plain is destined to be the source of the world's supply of soya bean. Besides soya bean, this plain also produces a great quantity of various kinds of grains, and supplies the entire Eastern Siberia with wheat. The Manchurian mountains are exceedingly rich in timber and minerals—gold being especially found in great quantities in many localities.

Railway construction in this region has proved to be a most profitable undertaking. At present there are already three railway systems tapping this rich country, viz., the Peking-Mukden line, the best paying railroad in China, the Japanese South-Manchurian Railway, also a very remunerative line, and the Chinese Eastern Railway, the best paying portion of the whole Siberian system. Besides these, there are many lines projected by the Japanese. In order to develop this rich region properly a network of railways should be projected.

Before dealing with the separate lines of this net-work of railways, I should like to propose a center for them, just as the spider's nest is to a cobweb. I shall name this central city "Tungchin," the Eastern Mart, which should be situated at a point southwest of the junction of the Sungari and Nonni rivers, about 100 miles west by south from Harbin, and will be in a more advantageous position than the latter. This new city will be the center not only of the railway system but also of the inland water communication when the Liaoho-Sungari Canal is completed.

With the projected city of Tungchin as a center, I propose the following lines:

    a. The Tungchin-Hulutao line.
    b. The Tungchin-Great Northern Port line.
    c. The Tungchin-Dolon Nor line.
    d. The Tungchin-Kerulen line.
    e. The Tungchin-Moho line.
    f. The Tungchin-Korfen line.
    g. The Tungchin-Yaoho line.
    h. The Tungchin-Yenchi line.
    i. The Tungchin-Changpeh line.
    j. The Hulutao-Jehol-Peking line.
    k. The Hulutao-Kerulen line.
    l. The Hulutao-Hailar line.
    m. The Hulutao-Antung line.
    n. The Moho-Suiyuan line.
    o. The Huma-Chilalin or Shihwei line.
    p. The Ussuri-Tumen-Yalu-Coast line.
    q. The Linkiang-Dolon Nor line.
    r. The Chikatobo-Sansing or Ilan line.

DEVELOPMENT OF CHINA 139

    s. The Sansing or Ilan-Kirin line.
    t. The Kirin-Dolon Nor line.

A. THE TUNGCHIN-HULUTAO LINE

This is the first line that radiates from this projected Manchurian railway center, and is the shorter of the two direct lines that lead to the ice-free ports on the Liaotung-Chihli Gulf. It runs almost parallel to the South Manchurian Railway, the distance between the two lines being about 80 miles at the northern end, converging to 40 miles at Sinmin, and diverging again after that point. According to the original agreement with the former Russian Government, no parallel line within 100 miles was allowed to be built. But such restriction must be abolished under this new International Development Scheme for the benefit of all concerned. This line starts from Tungchin, and proceeds southward across the vast Manchurian plain by Changling, Shuangshan, Liaoyuan, and Kangping, to Sinmin in a straight line covering a distance of about 270 miles. After Sinmin, the line joins the Peking-Mukden Railway and runs on the same track for a distance of about 130 miles to Hulutao.

B. THE TUNGCHIN-GREAT NORTHERN PORT LINE

This line is the second that radiates from this railway center direct to a deep water ice-free seaport. It starts from Tungchin, proceeding in a southwesterly direction, passes Kwangan, midway between Tungchin and the West Liaoho, and many other small settlements before it crosses the Liaoho. After crossing the Liaoho, it enters the mountainous regions of the Jehol district by a valley to Fowsin, a hsien city, and crosses the watershed into the Talingho Valley. After passing through the Talingho Valley, the line crosses another watershed into the Luan Valley by a branch of the same river. Then it penetrates the Great Wall and proceeds to the Great Northern Port by way of Yungping and Loting. The whole length of this line is about 550 miles, the first half of which is on level land and the second half in mountainous country.

C. THE TUNGCHIN-DOLON NOR LINE

This is the third line that radiates from the railway center and proceeds nearly in a westerly direction across the plain to Taonan where it crosses the projected Aigun-Jehol line (Japanese), and also meets the termini of two other projected lines, the Changchun-Taonan and the Tsengkiatun-Taonan (Japanese). After Taonan, the line turns more southward by skirting along the foothills of the southeastern side of the Great Khingan range where vast virgin forests and rich minerals are found. Then it passes through the upper Liaoho Valley formed by the Great Khingan Mountain on the north, and the Jehol Mountain on the south and through the towns of Linsi and Kingpang to Dolon Nor, where it meets the trunk line of the Northwestern Railway system. This line covers a distance of about 480 miles, a great part of which is on level land.

D. THE TUNGCHIN-KERULEN LINE

This is the fourth line that radiates from the Tungchin Railway center. It runs in a northwesterly direction almost parallel with the Harbin-Manchuli line of the Chinese Eastern Railway, the distance between the two lines varying from 100 to 130 miles. The line starts from Tungchin on the north side of the junction of the Nonni and Sungari rivers and proceeds westward across the Nonni River to Talai, and then turns northwestward across the plain into the valley of the north branch of the Guileli River. After entering the valley, it follows the stream up to its source, then crosses the Great Khingan Mountain watershed into the Mongolian Plain by the Khalka River, and follows the right bank of this river to the north end of Bor Nor Lake. Thence it turns directly westward to the Kerulen River, and follows the south bank of the river to Kerulen. This line covers a distance of about 630 miles.

E. THE TUNGCHIN-MOHO LINE

This is the fifth line that radiates from this railway center. It starts from the north side of the junction of the Nonni and Sungari rivers, and proceeds northwestward across the northern end of the Great Manchurian Plain to Tsitsiha. At Tsitsiha, it joins the projected Kinchow-Aigun line and proceeds together northwestward alongside the left bank of the Nonni River as far as Nunkiang where it separates from the other. Thence it resumes the northwesterly direction and proceeds into the upper Nonni Valley until the headwater is reached. Then it crosses the northern extremity of the Great Khingan Range to Moho, where it joins the terminus of the Dolon Nor-Moho line. This line is about 600 miles long. About a quarter of this length runs on the plain, the second quarter runs along the lower Nonni Valley, the third along the Upper Valley, and the fourth runs in mountainous but gold-bearing regions, where only physical difficulties are to be expected.

F. THE TUNGCHIN-KORFEN LINE

This is the sixth line from the railway center. It also starts on the northern side of the Nonni-Sungari junction, and proceeds across the plain by the cities Chaotung and Tsingkang. After Tsingkang it crosses the Tungkun River, proceeds to Hailun, and then, ascending the Tungkun Valley, crosses the watershed of the Little Khingan Mountain. Thence it descends into the Korfen Valley and proceeds by Chelu to Korfen on the right bank of the Amur River. This line covers a distance of 350 miles, two thirds of which run on comparatively level land and one third in mountainous district. This is the shortest line from Tungchin to the Amur River and the Russian territory on yonder side.

G. THE TUNGCHIN-YAOHO LINE

This is the seventh line that radiates from this railway center. It starts from the northern side of the Nonni-Sungari junction and traverses the plain on the left of the Sungari River by Chaochow, then crosses the Chinese Eastern Railway, and the Hulan River to Hulan. After Hulan, it proceeds to Payen, Mulan, and Tungho, then crosses the Sungari River to Sansing, now called Ilan. Thence it proceeds into the Wokan Valley and crosses the watershed by Chihsingshitse and Takokai into the Noloho Valley and passing by various villages and towns along this river to Yaohohsien, ends at the junction of the Noloho and the Ussuri River. This line covers a distance of 500 miles in very fertile country.

H. THE TUNGCHIN-YENCHI LINE

This is the eighth line that radiates from this railway center. It starts from the eastern side of the Nonni-Sungari junction and proceeds in a southeasterly direction on the right side of he Sungari River to Fuyu or Petunai and various towns along the road on the same side of the river until it comes across the Harbin-Talien Railway, then turns away from the road and proceeds eastward to Yushu and Wuchang. After Wuchang, the line turning more southward, proceeds to Fengtechang and then follows the same direction to Omu. At Omu, it crosses the Mutan River, then proceeds to Liangshuichuan and Shehtauho, where it joins the Japanese Hweining-Kirin line and proceeds together to Yenchi. This line covers a length of about 330 miles through very rich agricultural and mineral country.

I. THE TUNGCHIN-CHANGPEH LINE

This is the ninth line that radiates from the Tungchin railway center. It starts from the south side of the Nonni-Sungari junction and proceeds in a southeasterly direction across the plain to Nungan. After Nungan, it crosses the Itung River and proceeds continuously in the same direction across several branches of the same river to Kiudaichan, where it joins the Changchun-Kirin line and proceeds together as far as Kirin. After Kirin, it goes its own way following the right bank of the Sungari River in a southeasterly direction to the junction of Lafaho River and turns southward along the same bank of the Sungari to Huatien. After Huatien, it continues in the same course up to Toutaokiang, as far as Fusung, then turns southeastward into the Sunghsiangho Valley and proceeds upward to the

Changpeh Shan watershed by skirting the south side of the Celestial Lake, then turns southward following the Aikiang River to Changpeh on the Korean frontier. This line covers a distance of about 330 miles. Some great difficulties are to be overcome in the last portion of the line where it crosses the Changpeh watershed.

J. THE HULUTAO-JEHOL-PEKING LINE

With this line I shall begin to deal with a new group of the Northeastern Railway System which will make Hulutao, the ice-free port on the Liaotung Gulf as their center and terminus. This, the first line, starts from Hulutao and proceeds westward up the Shaho Valley to Sintaipienmen. Thence it crosses the mountainous district through Haiting, Mangniuyingtse, and Sanshihkiatse to Pingchuan, and continues in the same direction to Jehol or Chengteh. After Jehol, it proceeds by the old imperial highway to Lwanping, then turns southwestward to Kupehkow where it penetrates the Great Wall. Thence it follows the same highway through Miyun and Shunyi to Peking. This line covers a distance of about 270 miles.

K. THE HULUTAO-KERULEN LINE

This is the second line of the Hulutao radiation. It starts from this seaport and proceeds northward through the mountainous region of Jehol by Kienping and Chihfeng. Thence, the line follows the highway across the Upper Valley of Liaoho to Chianchang, Sitoo, Takinkou, and Linsi. After Linsi, it proceeds up the Lukiako Valley and crosses the watershed at the southern extremity of the Great Khingan Mountain, through Kanchumiao and Yufuchih. Then it proceeds to Payenbolak, Uniket, and Khombukure where it joins with the Dolon Nor-Kerulen line and proceeds together to Kerulen. This line up to Khombukure covers a distance of about 450 miles, tapping a very rich mineral, timber, and agricultural country.

L. THE HULUTAO-HAILAR LINE

This, the third line, starts from Hulutao and proceeds by way of Chinchow along the west side on the Talingho River to Yichow, where it crosses the Talingho to Chinghopienmen and Fowsin. After Fowsin, the line goes northward to Suitung, thence, crossing the Siliaoho to Kailu, it proceeds between the Great and Little Fish Lakes to Kinpan and Tachuan. Then it proceeds across the Great Khingan Mountain into the Oman Valley and follows the same river to Hailar. This line covers a distance of about 600 miles passing through rich mineral and agricultural land and virgin forests.

M. THE HULUTAO-ANTUNG LINE

This, the fourth line, starts from Hulutao and proceeding northeastward, follows the course of the projected Liaoho-Hulutao Canal, and then goes eastward to Newchwang and Haicheng. From there it proceeds southeastward to Sinmuchen, where it joins the Antung-Mukden line and proceeds together to Antung on the Korean border. This line covers a distance of about 220 miles. This together with the Hulutao-Jehol-Peking line will make the shortest line from Antung and beyond, i. e., Korea, to Peking.

N. THE MOHO-SUIYUAN LINE

With this as the first I am going to deal with another group of lines in this system. These will be the circumferential lines which link up the radii from the Tungchin center in two semicircles, the outer and the inner. This Moho-Suiyuan line starts from Moho and proceeds along the right bank of the Amur River to Ussuri, Omurh, Panga, Kaikukang, Anlo, and Woshimen. After this point, the river bends more southward and the line follows the same bend to Ankan, Chahayen, Wanghata, and Huma. From Huma, it proceeds to Sierhkenchi, Chila, Manchutun, Heiho, and Aigun where it meets the terminus of the Chinchow-Aigun line. After Aigun, the line turns more eastward to Homolerhchin, Chilirh, and Korfen where it meets the terminus of the Tungchin-Korfen line. Thence it proceeds to Wuyun, Foshan, and Lopeh. After Lopeh, it goes to Hokang at the junction of the Amur and Sungari. At this point, the line crosses the Sungari River to Tungkiang and proceeds to Kaitsingkow, Otu, and Suiyuan where it ends. This line covers a distance of 900 miles running all its way through the gold-producing region.

O. THE HUMA-CHILALIN OR SHIHWEI LINE

This is merely a branch of the Moho-Suiyuan line. It starts from Huma and follows the Kumara River passing by the Taleitse Gold Mine and Wapalakow Gold Mine. Then it proceeds up the Kumara River in a westerly and southwesterly direction to its southern source and there it crosses the watershed into the Halarh Valley, thence descending the valley to Chilalin or Shihwei. This line covers a distance of about 320 miles running in an extremely rich gold district.

P. THE USSURI-TUMEN-YALU-COAST LINE

This, the second line of the outer semicircle, starts by continuing the first line at Suiyuan, and proceeds along the left bank of the Ussuri River, passing Kaulan, Fuyeu, and Minkang, to Yaoho, where it meets the terminus of the Tungchin-Yaoho line. From Yaoho, it runs parallel to the Russian Ussuri Railway on the east side of the river as far as Fulin. After Fulin, it parts from the Russian line by turning westward following the Mulingho River to Mishan on the northwestern corner of the Hanka Lake. Thence it goes to Pinganchin, turns southward alongside the boundary line and crosses the Harbin-Vladivostok line at Siusuifen Station to Tungning. After Tungning, it continues the same southward course alongside the boundary line to a point between Szetaukow and Wutaukow, then turns westward to Hunchun, and northwestward to Yenchi where it meets the projected Japanese Hweining-Kirin line. From Yenchi, it follows the Japanese line to Holung, and proceeds southwestward by the left side of the Tumen River across the watershed into the Yalu Valley, where it meets the Tungchin-Changpeh line. After Changpeh it turns westward and northwestward following the right bank of the Yalu to Linkiang, thence southwestward, still following the right bank of the Yalu, to Tsianhsien and then continues in the same direction, along the Yalu bank, to Antung, where it meets the Antung-Mukden Railway. After Antung, it proceeds to Tatungkow at the mouth of the Yalu, thence along the coast to Takushan and Chwangho, then westward through Situn and Pingfangtien to join the South Manchurian Railway at Wukiatun. This line covers a distance of 1,100 miles, which runs from end to end right along the southeastern boundary of Manchuria.

Q. THE LINKIANG-DOLON NOR LINE

This is the third line of the outer semicircle of the Tungchin railway center, and connects the radiating lines south of the center. It starts from Linkiang at the southwestward turn of the Yalu River, and proceeds across the mountainous region passing by Tunghwa, Hingking, and Fushun, to Mukden, where it crosses the South Manchurian Railway. From Mukden, it goes together with the Peking-Mukden line as far as Sinmin, where it crosses the Tungchin-Hulutao line and proceeds northwestward through Sinlihtun to Fowsin. After Fowsin the line enters the hilly district of the upper Liaoho Valley, and proceeds to Chihfeng, after passing through numerous small villages and camping places in this vast pasture. After Chihfeng the line proceeds through the Yinho Valley by Sanchotien, Kungchuling, and Tachientse, to Famuku, thence follows the Tulakanho to Dolon Nor, covering a distance of about 500 miles.

R. THE CHIKATOBO-SANSING OR ILAN LINE

This is the first line of the inner semicircle which connects the radiating lines from the Tungchin railway center on the northeast. It starts from Chikatobo on the upper reach of the Amur, and proceeds eastward and southeastward through many valleys and mountains of the Great Khingan Range to Nunkiang. After Nunkiang, it goes in a more southerly direction to Keshan, thence to Hailun, and then crosses the Sungari to Sansing or Ilan. This line covers a distance of about 700 miles, passing through an agricultural and gold-producing country.

S. THE SANSING OR ILAN-KIRIN LINE

This is the second line of the inner semicircle. It starts from Sansing and proceeds southwestward along the right bank of the Mutan River through Tauchan, Erchan, Sanchan, and Szuchan, to Chengtse where it crosses the Harbin-Vladivostok line. Then it goes to Ninguta, after crossing over the Mutan River from right to the left bank. After Ninguta it proceeds southwestward passing through Wungcheng, Lanchichan, Talachan, and Fungwangtien, to Omu. From Omu it joins the Japanese Hweining-Kirin line and proceeds westward to Kirin. This line covers a distance of about 200 miles, along the fertile Mutan Valley.

T. THE KIRIN-DOLON NOR LINE

This is the third line of the inner semicircle in the Tungchin system. It starts from Kirin and follows the old highway westward to Changchun where it meets the termini of the Chinese Eastern Railway from the north and the Japanese South Manchurian Railway from the south. After Changchun, it proceeds across the plain to Shuangshan where it meets the Tungchin-Hulutao line and the Japanese Szupingkai-Chengkiatun-Taonan line. From Shuangshan, it crosses the Liao River to Liaoyuan, thence it traverses the vast plain, crossing the Tungchin-Great Northern Port line and goes to Suitung where it meets the Hulutao-Hailar line. After Suitung, it proceeds up the Liao Valley where it comes across the Hulutao-Kerulen line and then crosses the watershed to Dolon Nor where it ends. This line covers a distance of 500 miles. This completes the cobweb system of the projected North-Eastern Railway. The total length of this entire system is about 9,000 miles.

PART IV

THE EXTENSION OF THE NORTHWESTERN RAILWAY SYSTEM

The Northwestern Railway System covers the region of Monogolia, Sinkiang, and a part of Kansu, an area of 1,700,000 square miles. This territory exceeds the area of the Argentine Republic by 600,000 square miles. Argentina is now the greatest source of the world's meat supply, while the Mongolian pasture is not yet developed, owing to the lack of transportation facilities. As Argentina has superseded the United States in supplying the world with meat, so the Mongolian pasture will some day take the place of Argentina, when railways are developed and cattle raising is scientifically improved. Thus the construction of railroads in this vast food-producing region is an urgent necessity as a means of relieving the world from food shortage. In the first program of this International Development Scheme, I proposed 7,000 miles of railways for this vast and fertile region, for the purpose of developing the Great Northern Port, and relieving the congested population of southeastern China. But this 7,000 miles of railways form merely a pioneer line. In order to develop this virgin continent properly, more railways have to be constructed. Therefore in this plan, namely, the Extension of the Northwestern Railway System, I propose the following lines:

a. The Dolon Nor-Kiakata line.
b. The Kalgan-Urga-Tannu Ola line.
c. The Suiyuan-Uliassutai-Kobdo line.
d. The Tsingpien-Tannu Ola line.
e. The Suchow-Kobdo line.
f. The Northwestern Frontier line.
g. The Tihwa or Urumochi-Ulankom line.

DEVELOPMENT OF CHINA

h. The Gaskhiun-Tannu Ola line.
i. The Uliassutai-Kiakata line.
j. The Chensi or Barkul-Urga line.
k. The Suchow-Urga line.
l. The Desert Junction-Kerulen line.
m. The Khobor-Kerulen-Chikatobo line.
n. The Wuyuan-Taonan line.
o. The Wuyuan-Dolon Nor line.
p. The Yenki-Ili line.
q. The Ili-Hotien line.
r. The Chensi-Kashgar line and its branches.

A. THE DOLON-KIAKATA LINE

This line starts from Dolon Nor and proceeds in a northwesterly direction, following the caravan road across the vast pasture to Khorkho, Kuoto, and Suliehto. After Suliehto, it crosses the boundary line into Outer Mongolia by the same road to Khoshentun, Lukuchelu, and Yangto. Thence it crosses the Kerulen River to Otukunkholato, and enters the hilly region where it crosses the Kerulen watershed and the Chikoi watershed. The water from the Kerulen watershed flows into the Amur, and thence into the Pacific Ocean, while the water from the Chikoi watershed flows into Lake Baikal, and thence to the Arctic Ocean. After crossing the Chikoi watershed, it follows a branch of the Chikoi River to Kiakata. This line covers a distance of about 800 mile.

B. THE KALGAN-URGA-TANNU OLA LINE

This line starts from Kalgan at the Great Wall, and proceeds northwestward up the plateau, crosses a range of hills into the Mongolian prairie, and goes to Mingan, Boroldshi, Ude, and Khobor, where it crosses the Dolon Nor-Urumochi trunk line. After Khobor, it proceeds across the vast and rich pasture of Mubulan, then proceeds in a straight line through Mukata and Nalaiha to Urga. From Urga, it goes into the hilly district crossing Selenga Valley to a point opposite the southern end of Lake Kos Gol, and then turns northward across a range of mountains to Khatkhyl on the southern shore of Kos Gol. After Khatkhyl, it skirts Kos Gol Lake along the western shore for some distance, then turns northwestward and westward, following the course of the Khua Kem River to a point near its exit at the frontier line, then turns southwestward up the Kemtshik Valley to its headwater, passes through Pakuoshwo, and ends at the boundary line between the Russian and Chinese territories. This line covers a distance of about 1,700 miles.

C. THE SUIYUAN-ULIASSUTAI-KOBDO LINE

This line starts from Suiyuan in the northwestern corner of Shansi, and proceeds in a northwesterly direction across the hilly country into the Mongolian pasture to Tolibulyk, where it crosses the Great Northern Port-Hami line, and the Great Eastern Port-Urga line. After Tolibulyk, it proceeds in a straight line in the same direction passing through Barunsudshi to the capital of Tuchetu. Thence it continues in the same straight line northwestward to Gorida. After Gorida, it follows the caravan road to Kolitikolik where it crosses the Great Northern Port-Urumochi trunk line. From Kolitikolik, the line turns northwestward, then westward and proceeds across many streams and valleys and passes by many small towns to Uliassutai. At Uliassutai, it crosses the B. Junction-Frontier branch of the Great Eastern Port-Urumochi line. After Uliassutai, the line pro-

DEVELOPMENT OF CHINA

ceeds westward following the trade road, passes through Khuduku, Bogu, Durganor, and Sakhibuluk to Kobdo. Thence the line turns northwestward to Khonga, Ukha, and Clegei, then westward to Beleu and ends at the frontier. This line is about 1,500 miles long.

D. THE TSINGPIEN-TANNU OLA LINE

This line starts from Tsingpien at the Great Wall, on the northern border of Shensi, proceeds through the Ordos country by Bonobalgasun, Orto, and Shinchao, and then crosses the Hoangho to Santaoho. From Santaoho, it proceeds across Charanarinula Mountain into Mongolian prairie in a northwesterly direction to Kurbansihata where it crosses the Peking-Hami line, then it goes to Unikuto and Enkin, where it crosses the Great Northern Port-Urumochi line. After Enkin, the line enters into a valley and watered district, proceeds northward to Karakorum, and then turns northwestward across various streams and valleys of the tributary of the Selenga River by Sabokatai and Tsulimiau. After Tsulimiau, it proceeds in the same direction across the Selenga River, follows its branch, the Telgir Morin River, up to its source and crosses the watershed into Lake Teri Nor. Then it follows the outlet of the Teri Nor to the Khua Kem River, where it ends by joining the Kalgan Urga-Tannu Ola line. This line covers a distance of about 1,200 miles.

E. THE SUCHOW-KOBDO LINE

This line starts from Suchow in a northwesterly direction penetrating the Great Wall at Chiennew, and proceeds to the coal field, about 150 miles from Suchow. Then it goes to Habirhaubuluk and Ilatoli. A short way from this place the line comes across the Peking-Hami line and then proceeds to Balaktai. After this the line passes a bit of pure desert to Timenchi. After entering the hilly and watered country it proceeds to Gaskhiun where it crosses the Great Northern Port-Urumochi trunk line. After Gaskhiun, it proceeds to Wolanhutok, Tabateng, and Tabutu where it joins the Kucheng and Kobdo highway and following it, proceeds to Kobdo, through Batokuntai and Sutai. Here the line ends, covering a distance of about 700 miles.

F. THE NORTHWESTERN FRONTIER LINE

This line starts from Ili following the Urumochi-Ili line to Santai, on the eastern side of Zairam Lake, then proceeds northeastward by itself to Tuszusai on the west side of Ebi Lake. After Tuszusai it proceeds to Toli where it crosses the Central Trunk line, that is, the Great Eastern Port-Tarbogotai line. Thence it goes to Namukotai and Stolokaitai by passing through a vast forest and a rich coal field. From Stolokaitai, the line follows the highway and proceeds to Chenghwaszu, the capital of Altai province. Thence it crosses a mountain range by the Urmocaitu Pass into the Kobdo Valley, and follows the course of the Kobdo River to Beleu where it joins the Suiyuan-Kobdo line and proceeds to Clegei. From Clegei, it proceeds by itself to Tabtu via Usungola and Ulamkom. At Tabtu, it joins the other line again and proceeds together to the Khua Kem River in the Tannu Ola district. It then turns eastward ascending the river to the junction of the Bei Kem and Khua Kem rivers, then starts again on its own course, following the former river and proceeds up to its source in a northeasterly direction ending at the frontier. This line covers a distance of about 900 miles.

G. THE TIHWA OR URUMOCHI-ULANKOM LINE

This line starts from Tihwa following the Dolon Nor trunk line to Fowkang, then proceeds by its own route almost northward through Chipichuan to Khorchute. From Khorchute, it turns northeastward and proceeds across a hilly district to Kaiche, then to Turhuta, where it crosses a branch line from Junction C. of the Great Northern Port-Urumochi line. After Turhuta, it turns northward, proceeds up the Pakaningale Valley to Zehoshita, and then crosses the Tilikta Pass. Thence it turns northeastward proceeding across the newly cultivated country to Kobdo. After Kobdo, it proceeds through a fertile plateau, by crossing many rivers and skirting many lakes to Ulankom, where it ends by joining the Northwestern Frontier line. It covers a distance of about 550 miles.

H. THE GASKHIUN-TANNU OLA LINE

This line starts from Gaskhiun and proceeds northeastward across a hilly and watered country through Hatonhutuk and Talangjoleu, to Pornulu. After Pornulu, the line proceeds across the Sapkhyn Valley by Huchirtu and Porkho to Uliassutai where it meets the Suiyuan-Kobdo, and the Great Eastern Port-Uliassutai lines. After Uliassutai, the line proceeds northward to a quite new country by first crossing the headwaters of Selenga, then the headwaters of the Tess River. In the Tess Valley the line crosses a vast virgin forest. After emerging from this forest it proceeds northwestward across the watershed into the Khua

Kem Valley in Tannu Ola and ends by joining the Northwestern Frontier line. This line covers a distance of about 650 miles.

I. THE ULIASSUTAI-KAIKATA LINE

This line starts from Uliassutai and runs on the track of the Gaskhiun-Tannu Ola line, until it reaches the Eder River, a branch of the Selenga. Then, turning off eastward, it begins its own course and proceeds downward following the course of the Eder River, crossing the Tsingpien-Tannu Ola line, to the junction of this river with the Selenga. There it joins the Kalgan-Urga-Tannu Ola line and proceeds together eastward in the common track for some distance until the other line turns southeastward, when this line turns northeastward following the Selenga down to Kiakata. This line covers a distance of about 550 miles, running through a fertile valley.

J. THE CHENSI OR BARKUL-URGA LINE

This line starts from Chensi or Barkul and proceeds northeastward across a cultivated region through Tutaku to Urkesiat. After Urkesiat, it crosses the Suchow-Kobdo line, then traverses the vast pasture on the north side of the Gobi Desert to Suchi and Dalantura. Thence it turns more northward across the Great Eastern Port-Uliassutai line, and the Dolon Nor-Urumochi line to Tashunhutuk. After this point the line crosses the Suiyuan-Uliassutai line at Ologai and proceeds over the watershed into the Selenga Valley where it crosses the Tsingpien-Tannu Ola line at Sabokatai. From here it turns eastward across a hilly and watered region to Urga. This line covers a distance of about 800 miles.

K. THE SUCHOW-URGA LINE

This line starts from Suchow and proceeds by Kinta to Maumu, and then follows the Taoho or Edsina River, which waters this strip of oasis, to the lakes. Thence it crosses the Gobi Desert, where it meets the crossing lines of the Peking-Hami and the Great Eastern Port-Uliassutai railways and with them forms a common junction. From this junction it proceeds across desert and pasture lands to another railway crossing which is formed by the Suiyuan-Kobdo and Tsingpien-Tannu Ola lines, also forming a common junction together. Thence it proceeds into pasture land through Hatengtu and Tolik to Sanintalai, where it crosses the Dolon Nor-Urumochi line. After Sanintalai, the line proceeds through Ulanhoshih and many other small towns and encampments to Urga. This line covers a distance of about 700 miles. One third of this length is through the desert and the other two thirds through watered pasture land.

L. THE DESERT JUNCTION-KERULEN LINE

This line starts from the Desert Junction, proceeds northeastward to the pastural land and crosses the Tsingpien-Tannu Ola line south of Ulan Nor Lake. Thence it proceeds to the Tuchetu Capital where it crosses the Suiyuan-Kobdo line. After the Tuchetu Capital it goes across a pasture to Junction A. From Junction A. it proceeds to Ulanhutuk and Chientingche, then crosses the Kalgan-Tannu Ola line to Zesenkhana. From Zesenkhana, the line follows the course of the Kerulen River down in a northeasterly direction to the city of Kerulen, where it crosses the Dolon Nor-Kerulen line, and meets the Kerulen-Tungchin line. This line covers a distance of about 800 miles.

M. THE KHOBOR-KERULEN-CHIKATOBO LINE

This line starts from Khobor, the crossing junction of the Dolon Nor-Urumochi, and the Kalgan-Urga-Tannu Ola lines, and proceeds northeastward across a vast pasture to Khoshentun, where it crosses the Dolon Nor-Kiakata line. After Khoshentun, it proceeds in the same direction across a similar pasture to Kerulen, where it crosses the Dolon Nor-Kerulen line. Then it proceeds first along the right bank of the Kerulen River, then crosses to the left side, and passes along the northwestern side of Hulan Lake. After Hulan Lake, the line crosses the Chinese Eastern Railway, and the Arguna River, then proceeds along the right bank of the river to Chikatobo, where the line ends by joining the Dolon Nor-Moho and the Chikatobo-Sansing lines. This line covers a distance of about 600 miles. The first half of it runs on dry land and the second half on watered land.

N. THE WUYUAN-TAONAN LINE

This line starts from Wuyuan at the northwest bend of the Hoangho and proceeds northeastward across the Sheiten Ula Mountain and pasture to Tolibulyk, where it meets the crossing junction of three lines—the Peking-Hami line, the Suiyuan-Kobdo line, and the Great Eastern Port-Urga line. From Tolibulyk the line proceeds continuously in the same direction across a pasture to Khobor where it meets the crossing junction of the Dolon Nor-Urumochi and the Peking-Urga lines, and also the terminus of the Khobor-

Kerulen line. After Khobor the line turns more eastward and runs across the Dolon Nor-Kiakata line midway to Khombukure, where it crosses the Dolon Nor-Kerulen and the Hulutao-Kerulen lines. From Khombukure the line proceeds to Dakmusuma, where it crosses the Dolon Nor-Moho line. Thence it goes eastward across the Great Khingan Mountain to Tuchuan, then turns southeastward to Taonan, where it ends. This line covers a distance of about 900 miles.

O. THE WUYUAN-DOLON NOR LINE

This line starts from Wuyuan and proceeds northeastward across the Sheiten Ula Mountain to Maomingan, where it crosses the Great Eastern Port-Urga line. Then it proceeds across the vast pasture and the Suiyuan-Kobdo line to Bombotu, where it passes over the Peking-Hami line. After Bombotu, the line turns eastward and proceeds across the Kalgan-Urga-Tannu Ola line, then goes to Dolon Nor, where it ends by joining the Dolon Nor-Mukden-Linkiang line, which forms a direct route from the upper Hoangho Valley to the rich Liaoho Valley. This line covers a distance of about 500 miles.

P. THE YENKI-ILI LINE

This line starts from Yenki or Karashar, and proceeds northwestward across the mountain pass into the Ili Valley. It then follows the Kunges River downward, in a westerly direction, traversing a most fertile valley, to Ining and Kuldja or Ili, the principal city of the Ili district near the Russian border, where it joins the Ili-Urumochi line. This line covers a distance of about 400 miles.

Q. THE ILI-HOTIEN LINE

This line starts from Ili or Kuldja, proceeds southward across the Ili River, then eastward along the left side of the river and then southeastward and southward to Bordai. From here it turns southwestward into Tekes Valley and proceeding upward crosses the Tekes River to Tienchiao and then ascends the mountain pass. After the mountain pass the line turns southeastward, traverses a vast coal field and then turns southwestward to Shamudai, where it crosses the Turfan-Kashgar line. From Shamudai it turns southward across the fertile zone of the north side of the Tarim Valley, to Bastutakelak. Then it proceeds southwestward to Hotien passing by on the way many small settlements in the fertile zone of the Hotien River which flows across the desert. At Hotien the line meets the Kashgar-Iden line. After Hotien the line proceeds upward to the highland south of the city and ends at the frontier. This line covers a distance of about 700 miles.

R. THE CHENSI-KASHGAR LINE AND ITS BRANCHES

This line starts from Chensi and proceeds southwestward along the Tienshan pasture through Yenanpoa, Shihkialoong, and Taolaitse to Chikoching, then along the Tienshan forest through Wutungkwo, Tungyenchi, Siyenchi, and Olong to Sensien, where it crosses the Central Trunk line. After Sensien it proceeds along the northern edge of the Tarim Desert through Lakesun City and Shehchuan to Hora, where it crosses the Cherchen-Koria line. From Hora the line proceeds along the course of the Tarim River, passing by many new settlements, fertile regions, and virgin forests, to Bastutakelak, where it crosses the Ili-Hotien line.

DEVELOPMENT OF CHINA 161

Thence it goes through Pachu to Kashgar where it meets the Urumochi-Iden line. After Kashgar it proceeds northwestward to the frontier where it ends. Attached to this line are two branches. The first branch proceeds from Hora southwestward through many oases to Cherchen. The second proceeds from Pachu southwestward along the Yarkand River to Sache and then westward to Puli near the frontier. This line including the branches covers a distance of about 1,600 miles. The total length of this entire system is about 16,000 miles. See general map.

PART V

THE HIGHLAND RAILWAY SYSTEM

This, the last part of my railway program, is the most difficult and most expensive undertaking of its kind; consequently, it must be the least remunerative of all the railway enterprises in China. So no work should be attempted in this part until all the other parts are fully developed. But when all the other parts are well equipped with railways then railway construction in this highland region will also be remunerative, despite the difficulties and the highly expensive work in construction.

The highland region consists of Tibet, Kokonor, and a part of Sinkiang, Kansu, Szechwan, and Yunnan, an area of a about 1,000,000 square miles. Tibet is known to be the richest country in the world for gold deposits. Furthermore the adjacent territories possess rich agricultural and pastural lands. This vast region is little known to the outside world. The Chinese call Tibet "the Western Treasury," for, besides gold, there are other kinds of metals especially copper, in great quantities. Indeed the name of the Western Treasury is most appropriately applied to this unknown region. When the world's supply of precious metals are exhausted, we have to resort to this vast mineral bearing region for supply. So railways will be necessary at least for mining purposes. I therefore propose the following lines:

    a. The Lhasa-Lanchow line.
    b. The Lhasa-Chengtu line.
    c. The Lhasa-Tali-Cheli line.
    d. The Lhasa-Taklongshong line.
    e. The Lhasa-Yatung line.
    f. The Lhasa-Laichiyaling line.
    g. The Lhasa-Nohho line.
    h. The Lhasa-Iden line.
    i. The Lanchow-Chochiang line.
    j. The Chengtu-Dzunsasak line.
    k. The Ningyuan-Cherchen line.
    l. The Chengtu-Menkong line.
    m. The Chengtu-Yuankiang line.
    n. The Suifu-Tali line.
    o. The Suifu-Mengting line.
    p. The Iden-Gortok line.

A. THE LHASA-LANCHOW LINE

This is the most important line of this system for it connects the capital city of Tibet—a vast secluded region with several millions of people—with the central trunk line of the country. The route which it passes through is inhabitable and is already slightly inhabited in the region between the ends of the proposed line. So it will probably

DEVELOPMENT OF CHINA 163

be a paying line from the beginning. This line starts from Lhasa, following the old imperial highway in a northward direction and proceeds by Talong to Yarh, which lies on the southeastern side of Tengri Nor Lake. After Yarh, the line turns more eastward and proceeds across the watershed from the Sanpo Valley to the Lukiang Valley by the Shuangtsu Pass. Thence turning more eastward the line proceeds across the headwater of the Lukiang to that of the Yangtze by passing many valleys, streams, and mountain passes. Then it crosses the main body of the Upper Yangtze, which is here known as the Kinshakiang, over the Huhusair Bridge. After crossing the bridge, it turns southeastward, then eastward across the Yangtze Valley into the Hoangho Valley, where it passes through many small towns and encampments into the Starry Sea region. At the Starry Sea, the line passes between the lakes of Oring Nor and Tsaring Nor. Thence it turns northeastward across the southeast valley of the Zaidam region, and returns into the Hoangho Valley again. Then it proceeds through Katolapo and various towns to Dangar, now called Hwangyuan, situated near the border between Kansu and Kokonor. After Dangar, the line turns southeastward following the course of the Sining River, proceeds downward through a very rich valley and passes through Sining, Nienpai, and hundreds of small towns and villages to Lanchow. This line covers a distance of 1,100 miles.

B. THE LHASA-CHENGTU LINE

This line starts from Lhasa and proceeds northeastward on the former imperial highway by Teking and Nanmo to Motsukungchia. Thence it turns southeastward and northeastward to Giamda. From Giamda, the line turns northward, then northeastward where it proceeds through the Tolala Pass to Lhari. After Lhari the line goes in an easterly direction and passes Pianpa, Shihtuh, and many small towns to Lolongchong. Thence it crosses the Lukiang by the Kayu Bridge and then turns northeastward to Kinda and Chiamdo. After Chiamdo, the line instead of following the imperial highway southeastward to Batang, turns northeastward, following another trade route, and proceeds to Payung at the northwestern corner of Szechwan. From Payung, it proceeds across the Kinshakiang over the bridge near Sawusantusze. The line then turns southeastward, enters the Ichu Valley and proceeds downward to Kantzu on the Yalung River. Thence it proceeds to Chango and Yinker, to Badi on the Great Golden River, and Mongan on the Little Golden River. After Mongan, the line goes through the Balan Pass to Kwanhsien, and entering the Chengtu Plain, reaches Chengtu by Pihsien. This line covers a distance of about 1,000 miles.

C. THE LHASA-TALI-CHELI LINE

This line starts from Lhasa by the same track as the Lhasa-Chengtu line as far as Giamda. From Giamda, it proceeds by its own track southeastward, following a branch of the Sanpo River to Yulu, where this branch joins its main stream. After Yulu, it follows the left bank of the Sanpo River passing by Kongposaga to Timchao. From Timchao, the line turns away from the Sanpo River and proceeds in an eastward direction to Timchong city, Ikung, Kuba, and Shuachong. After Shuachong, the line proceeds southeastward to Lima, thence eastward to Menkong on the Lukiang. From Menkong, the line turns southward and goes along the right bank of the Lukiang passing Samotung to Tantau. Then crossing the Lukiang, it proceeds across the watershed through Gaiwa village to the Lantsang (or Mekong) River, and to Hsiaoweisi beyond it. After Hsiaoweisi, it follows the river bank to the Chenghsin Copper Mine, thence it turns away from the river and proceeds by Hosi, Erhyuan, Tengchow, and Shangkwang to Tali. From Tali, the line proceeds to Hsiakwang, Fengyi, Menghwa, and then meets the Lantsang River again at Paotien. Thence it follows the left bank southward right through to Cheli, where it ends. This line covers a distance of 900 miles.

D. THE LHASA-TAKLONGSHONG LINE

This line starts from Lhasa and proceeds southward by way of Teking to the Sanpo River where turning eastward it follows the left bank of the river to Sakorshong. After crossing the Sanpo River to Chetang, it proceeds southward by Chikablung, Menchona, Tawang, Dhirangjong to Taklongshong and continues farther on until it reaches the Assam frontier. This line covers a distance of 200 miles.

E. THE LHASA-YATUNG LINE

This line starts from Lhasa and proceeds southwestward by Chashih following the former imperial highway by Yitang and Kiangli to Chushui. At Chushui, it crosses to Sanpo River over the Mulih Bridge to Chakamo on the south side, thence to Tamalung, Paiti, Tabolung, and Nagartse. After Nagartse, the line turns westward to Jungku, Lhaling, and Shachia. At Shachia, the line leaves the former imperial highway and turns southwestward again and proceeds via Kula to Yatung at the Sikkim border. This line covers a distance of 250 miles.

F. THE LHASA-LAICHIYALING LINE AND BRANCHES

This line starts from Lhasa and proceeds northwestward by Chashih following the former imperial road to Little Taking, and westward to Yangpachin and Sangtolohai. Thence turning southwestward, it proceeds to Namaling and Tangto, and crosses the Sanpo River at Lhaku. After Lhaku, the line turns westward to Shigatse, the second important city in Tibet whence it proceeds in the same direction to Chashihkang, Pangcholing, and Lhatse all on the right side of the Sanpo River. From Lhatse, a branch line starts southwestward via Chayakor and Dingri to Niehlamuh on the Nepal border. The main line, however, crosses to the left side of the Sanpo River and proceeds on the same highway via Nabringtaka to Tadum where another branch line proceeds southwestward to the Nepal border. The main line continues northwestward via Tamusa and Choshan to Gartok, thence turning westward it proceeds to Laichiyaling on the Sutlej River and ends on the Indian border. This line, including the two branches, covers a distance of 850 miles.

G. THE LHASA-NOHHO LINE

This line starts from Lhasa and runs in the same track as line (f) to Sangtolohai where it proceeds by its own line northwestward to Teching, Sangchashong, and Taktung. Thence, it enters into the richest gold field in Tibet and through Wengpo, Tulakpa, Kwangkwei, and Ikar reaches Nohho, where the line ends. It covers a distance of 700 miles.

DEVELOPMENT OF CHINA 167

H. THE LHASA-IDEN LINE

This line starts from Lhasa, following the common track of lines (f) and (g) to the southwestern corner of Tengri Lake, whence it proceeds by its own track northwestward by Lungmajing, Tipoktolo and four or five other small places to Sari. After Sari, the line penetrates a vast tract of uninhabited land to Pakar and Suketi. Thence crossing the mountain passes and descending from the highland to the Tarim Basin through Sorkek to Yasulakun, the line joins the Cherchen-Iden railway of the Northwestern System and proceeds on the same track to Iden. This line covers a distance of 700 miles.

I. THE LANCHOW-CHOCHIANG LINE

This line starts from Lanchow, on the same track of the Lhasa-Lanchow line as far as the southeastern corner of the Lake Kokonor. Thence it proceeds on its own track by skirting along the southern shore of Lake Kokonor to Dulankit, where it turns southwestward to Dzunsasak. From Dzunsasak, the line proceeds in a westerly course along the southern side of the Zaidam Swamp, and passes Tunyueh, Halori, and Golmot to Hatikair. After Hatikair, the line turns northwestward by Baipa, Nolinjoha, to Orsinte. Thence turning more northward, it proceeds across the mountain range by Tsesinvitusuik and Tuntunomik to Chochiang, where it ends by joining the Ansi-Iden and Chochiang-Koria lines, covering a distance of 700 miles.

J. THE CHENGTU-DZUNSASAK LINE

This line starts from Chengtu and proceeds to Kwanhsien on the track of the Lhasa-Chengtu line, thence northward on its own track by Wenchuan, to Mauchow. Then, it proceeds northwestward following the course of the Minkiang to Sungpan. After Sungpan, it ascends the Min Valley passing Tungpi to Shangleyao, where it crosses the watershed from the Yangtze River side to that of the Hoangho. Thence the line proceeds to Orguseri, and following a branch of the Hoangho to the northwestern turn of its main stream, it proceeds along its right bank via Chahuntsin to Peilelachabu. There it crosses the Hoangho to the northwest turn of the old imperial road, where it joins the Lhasa-Lanchow line and proceeds as far as Lanipar. Then turning northwestward, it proceeds by its own line to Dzunsasak, where it ends by joining the Lanchow-Chochiang line. This line covers a distance of 650 miles.

K. THE NINGYUAN-CHERCHEN LINE

This line starts from Ningyuan and proceeds in a northwestward direction via Hwaiyuanchen to the Yalungkiang. Then it ascends along the left side of that river to Yakiang, and crossing to the right side of that river it proceeds by the old post road to Siolo, where it turns away from the river and follows the same post road to Litang. From Litang it proceeds in the same direction but follows another road to Kangtu, on the left side of the Kinshakiang. Following the same side of the river, it proceeds to Sawusantusze, where it crosses the Lhasa-Chengtu line. After Sawusantusze, the line continues in the same direction and follows the same side of the Kinshakiang via Tashigompa, to the Huhusair Bridge, where it crosses the Lhasa-Lanchow line. Then following a northern branch of the Kinshakiang to its source and crossing the watershed, it proceeds along the caravan road by Hsinszukiang and Olokung to Cherchen, where it ends, covering a distance of about 1,350 miles. This is the longest line of this system.

L. THE CHENGTU-MENKONG LINE

This line starts from Chengtu and proceeds southwestward by Shuangliu, Hsintsin, Mingshan, to Yachow. From Yachow, it turns northwestward and proceeds to Tienchuan, then westward to Tatsienlu, Tunyolo, and Litang. After Litang, the line proceeds southwestward through Batang and Yakalo, to Menkong, covering a distance of about 400 miles of very mountainous country.

M. THE CHENGTU-YUANKIANG LINE

This line starts from Chengtu on the same track of the Chengtu-Menkong line, proceeds to Yachow and thence by its own track in the same direction via Jungching, to Tsingliu. After Tsingliu, the line proceeds southward through Yuehsi to Ningyuan, where it meets the head of the Ningyuan-Cherchen line. After Ningyuan, it goes to Kwaili, then crosses the Kinshakiang to Yunnanfu where it crosses the Canton-Tali line. From Yunnanfu, it proceeds along the west side of the Kunming Lake to Kunyang, and through Hsinshing, Hsingo, to Yuankiang, where the line ends by joining the Canton-Szemo line. It covers a distance of about 600 miles.

N. THE SUIFU-TALI LINE

This line starts from Suifu and proceeds along the left bank of the Yangtze River to Pingshan and Lupo. After

Lupo, it turns away from the river in a southwesterly direction and scales the Taliangshan Mountains to Ningyuan, where it crosses the Chengtu-Yuankiang line and meets the termini of the Canton-Ningyuan line and the Ningyuan-Cherchen line. Thence continuing in the same direction, it crosses the Yalungkiang to Yenyuan and Yungpeh. After Yungpeh, the line turns more southward, across the Kinshakiang to Sincheng and thence to Tali, where it ends by meeting the Canton-Tali line and the Lhasa-Tali line. It covers a distance of about 400 miles.

O. THE SUIFU-MENGTING LINE

This line starts from Suifu on the same track as the Suifu-Tali line as far as Lupo. From Lupo, it goes on its own track across the Yangtze River here known as the Kinshakiang, and follows the right side of that river upward to its southward bend where it crosses the Chengtu-Yuankiang line, to Yuanmow. From Yuanmow, it proceeds to Tsuyung, where it crosses the Canton-Tali line, thence to Kingtung. After Kingtung, it proceeds southwestward across the Lantsangkiang or Mekong River, to Yunchow, thence turning southwestward, it follows a branch of the Lukiang River to Mengting and ends on the frontier. This line covers a distance of about 500 miles.

P. THE IDEN-GARTOK LINE

This line starts from Iden, and proceeds southward along the Keriya River to Polu, thence following the caravan road up the highland to Kuluk. From Kuluk, it proceeds southwestward via Alasa and Tunglong to Nohho, where it meets the terminus of the Lhasa-Nohho line. After Nohho, it skirts around the eastern end of the Noh-tso-Lake to Rudok and proceeds southwestward to Demchok, on the Indus River. From Demchok, it proceeds southeastward following the Indus River up to Gartok, where it ends by joining the Lhasa-Laichiyaling line. This line covers a distance of about 500 miles. This highland system totals about 11,000 miles.

PART VI

THE ESTABLISHMENT OF LOCOMOTIVE AND CAR FACTORIES

The railways projected in the Fourth Program will total about 62,000 miles; and those in the First and the Third Programs about 14,000 miles. Besides these, there will be double tracks in the various trunk lines, which will make up a grand total of no less than 100,000 miles, as stated in the preliminary part of these programs. With this 100,000 miles of railways to be constructed in the coming ten years, the demands for locomotives and cars will be tremendous. The factories of the world will be unable to supply them, especially at this juncture of reconstruction after the great world war. So the establishment of locomotive and car factories in China to supply our own demands of railway equipment will be a necessary as well as a profitable undertaking. China possesses unlimited supplies of raw materials and cheap labor. What we need for establishing such factories is foreign capital and experts. What amount of capital should be invested in this project I have to leave to experts to decide.

I suggest that four large factories should be started simultaneously at the beginning—two on the coast and two on the Yangtze. Of those on the coast, one should be at the Great Northern Port, and the other at the Great Southern Port—Canton. Of those on the Yangtze, one should be at Nanking and the other at Hankow. All four are in centers of both land and water communication, where skilled labor can easily be obtained. They are also near our iron and coal fields. Besides these four great factories, others should be established at suitable centers of iron and coal fields when our railways will be more developed.

All the factories should be under one central control. The locomotives and cars of our future railways should be standardized so as to make possible the interchange of parts of machinery and equipment. We should also adopt the standard gauge, that is, the 4 feet 8½ inch gauge which has been adopted by most of the railways of the world. In fact, almost all the railways hitherto built in China are of this gauge. The purpose of the proposed standardization is to secure the highest efficiency as well as the greatest economy.

PROGRAM V

In the preceding four programs, I dealt exclusively with the development of the key and basic industries. In this one, I am going to deal with the development of the *main* group of industries which need foreign help. By the main group of industries, I mean those industries which provide every individual and family with the necessaries and comforts of life. Of course, when the key and basic industries are developed, the various other industries will spontaneously spring up all over the country, in a very short time. This had been the case in Europe and America after the industrial revolution. The development of the key and the basic industries will give plenty of work to the people and will raise their wages as well as their standard of living. When wages are high, the price for necessaries and comforts of life will also be increased. So the rise in wages will be accompanied by the rise in the cost of living. Therefore, the aim of the development of some of the main group of industries is to help reduce the high cost of living when China is in the process of international development, by giving to the majority of the people plenty of the essentials and comforts of life as well as higher wages.

It is commonly thought that China is the cheapest country to live in. This is a misconception owing to the common notion of measuring everything by the value of money. If we measure the cost of living by the value of labor then it will be found that China is the most expensive country for a common worker to live in. A Chinese coolie, a muscular worker, has to work 14 to 16 hours a day in order to earn a bare subsistence. A clerk in a shop, or a teacher in a village school cannot earn more than a hundred dollars a year. And the farmers after paying their rents and exchanging for a few articles of need with their produce have to live from hand to mouth. Labor is very cheap and plentiful but food and commodities of life are just enough to go round for the great multitude of the four hundred millions in China in an ordinary good year. In a bad year, a great number succumb to want and starvation. This miserable condition among the Chinese proletariat is due to the non-development of the country, the crude methods of production and the wastefulness of labor. The radical cure for all this is industrial development by foreign capital and experts for the benefit of the whole nation. Europe and America are a hundred years ahead of us in industrial development; so in order to catch up in a very short time we have to use their capital, mainly their machinery. If foreign capital cannot be gotten, we will have to get at least their experts and inventors to make for us our own machinery. In any case, we must use machinery to assist our enormous man-power to develop our unlimited resources.

In modern civilization, the material essentials of life are five, namely: food, clothing, shelter, means of locomotion, and the printed page. Accordingly I will formulate this program as follows:

  I. The Food Industry.
  II. The Clothing Industry.
  III. The Housing Industry.
  IV. The Motoring Industry.
  V. The Printing Industry.

PART I

THE FOOD INDUSTRY

The food industry should be treated under the following headings:

a. The Production of Food.
b. The Storage and Transportation of Food.
c. The Preparation and Preservation of Food.
d. The Distribution and Exportation of Food.

A. THE PRODUCTION OF FOOD

Human foods are derived from three sources: the land, the sea and the air. By far the most important and greatest in quantity consumed is aerial food of which oxygen is the most vital element. But this aerial food is abundantly provided by nature, and no human labor is needed for its production except that which is occasionally needed for the airman and the submariner. So this food is free to all. It is not necessary for us to discuss it here. The production of food from the sea which I have already touched upon when I dealt with the construction of fishing harbors and the building of fishing crafts, will also be left out here. It is the specific industries in the production of food from land, which need foreign help that are to be discussed here.

China is an agricultural country. About four-fifths of its population is occupied in the work of producing food. The Chinese farmer is very skillful in intensive cultivation. He can make the land yield to its utmost capacity. But vast tracts of arable lands are lying waste in thickly populated districts for one cause or other. Some are due to lack of water, some to too much of it and some to the "dog in the manger" system,—the holding up of arable land sharks for higher rents and prices.

The land of the eighteen provinces alone is at present supporting a population of four hundred millions. Yet there is still room for development which can make this same area of land yield more food if the waste land be brought under cultivation, and the already cultivated land be improved by modern machinery and scientific methods. The farmers must be protected and encouraged by liberal land laws by which they can duly reap the fruits of their own labor.

In regard to the production of food in our international development scheme, two necessary undertakings should be carried out which will be profitable at the same time.

(1) A scientific survey of the land.

(2) The establishment of factories for manufacturing agricultural machinery and implements.

(1) A scientific survey of the land. China has never been scientifically surveyed and mapped out. The administration of land is in the most chaotic state and the taxation of land is in great confusion, thus causing great hardships on the poor peasants and farmers. So, under any circumstance, the survey of land is the first duty of the government to execute. But this could not be done without foreign help, owing to lack of funds and experts. Therefore, I suggest that this work be taken up by an international organization. This organization should provide the expenses of the work by a loan, and should carry out the work with the required

number of experts and equipment. How much will be the expenses for the survey and what is the amount of time required and how large an organization is sufficient to carry on the work, and whether aerial survey by aeroplanes be practical for this work are questions which I shall leave to experts to decide.

When the topographical survey is going on a geological survey may be carried out at the same time so as to economize expenses. When the survey work is done and the land of each province is minutely mapped out, we shall be able to readjust the taxation of the already cultivated and improved land. As regards the waste and uncultivated lands we shall be able to determine whether they are suitable for agriculture, for pasture, for forestry, or for mining. In this way, we can estimate their value and lease them out to the users for whatever production that is most suitable. The surplus tax of the cultivated land and the proceeds of waste land will be for the payment of the interest and principal of the foreign loan. Besides the eighteen provinces, we have a vast extent of agricultural and pastural lands in Manchuria, Mongolia, and Sinkiang, and a vast extent of pastural land in Tibet and Kokonor. They will have to be developed by extensive cultivation under the colonization scheme, which is alluded to in the first program.

(2) The establishment of factories for manufacturing agricultural machinery and implements. When the waste land is reclaimed, cultivated land improved and waste labor set to work on the land, the demands for agricultural machinery and implements will be very great. As we have cheap labor and plenty of iron and coal, it is better and cheaper for us to manufacture than to import the imple-

ments and machinery. For this purpose, much capital should be invested, and factories should be put up in industrial centers or in the neighborhood of iron and coal fields, where labor and material could be easily found.

B. THE STORAGE AND TRANSPORTATION OF FOOD

The most important foodstuff to be stored and transported is grain. Under the present Chinese method, the storage of grain is most wasteful for if kept in large quantities it is often destroyed by insects or damaged by weather. It is only in small quantities and by great and constant care that grains can be preserved for a certain period of time. And the transportation of grains is also most expensive for the work is mostly done on man's shoulders. When the grains reach the waterway it is carried in a most makeshift way, without the least semblance of system. If the method of storing and transporting of grain be improved, a great economic saving could be accomplished. I propose that a chain of grain elevators be built all over the country and a special transport fleet be equipped all along the waterways by this International Development Organization. What will be the capital for this project and where the elevators should be situated have yet to be investigated by experts.

C. THE PREPARATION AND PRESERVATION OF FOOD

Hitherto the preparation of food is entirely by hand with a few primitive implements. The preservation of food is either by salt or sun heat. Mills and cannery method are scarcely known. I suggest that a system of rice mills should be constructed in all the large cities and towns in the Yangtze Valley and South China where rice is the staple food.

Flour mills should be put up in all large cities and towns north of the Yangtze Valley, where wheat, oats, and cereals other than rice are the staple food. All these mills should be under one central management so as to produce the best economic results. What amount of capital should be invested in this mill system by this international development scheme should be subjected to detailed investigation.

In regard to the preservation of food, fruits, meats and fishes should be preserved by canning or by refrigeration. If the canning industry is developed there will be created a great demand for tinplates. Therefore the establishment of tinplate factories will be necessary and also profitable. Such factories should be situated near the iron and tin fields. There are many localities in South China where tin, iron, and coal are situated near each other, thus providing ready materials for the factories. The tinplate factories and the canneries should be combined into one enterprise so as to secure best economic results.

D. THE DISTRIBUTION AND EXPORTATION OF FOOD

In ordinary good years, China never lacks food. There is a common saying in China that "One year's tilling will provide three years' wants." In the richer sections of the country, the people generally reserve three or four years' food supply in order to combat a bad year. But when China is developed and organized as an economic whole, one year's food reserve should be kept in the country for the use of the local people and the surplus should be sent out to the industrial centers. As the storage and transportation of food will be under a central management so the distribution and exportation of food should be under the same charge. All surplus grains of a country district should be sent to the nearest town for storage and each town or city should store one year's food. All the staple food should be sold only at cost price to the inhabitants according to their number, by the distributing department. And the surplus food should be exported to foreign countries where it is wanted and where the highest price can be obtained by the export department under the central management. Thus the surplus food will not be wasted as hitherto under the prohibition law. The proceeds of this export will surely amount to a huge sum which will be used in the payment of the interest and principal of the foreign loan invested in this undertaking.

We cannot complete this part of the food industry without giving special consideration to the tea and soya industries. The former, as a beverage, is well known throughout and used by the civilized world and the latter is just beginning to be realized as an important foodstuff by the scientists and food administrators. Tea, the most healthy and delicious beverage of mankind, is produced in China. Its cultivation and preparation form one of the most important industries of the country. Once China was the only country that supplied the world with tea. Now, China's tea trade has been wrested away from her by India and Japan. But the quality of the Chinese tea is still unequalled. The Indian tea contains too much tannic acid, and the Japanese tea lacks the flavor which the Chinese tea possesses. The best tea is only obtainable in China—the native land of tea. China lost her tea trade owing to the high cost of its production. The high cost of production is caused by the inland tax as well as the export duty and by the old methods of cultivation and preparation. If the tax and duty are done away with and new methods introduced, China can recover her former position in this trade easily. In this International Development Scheme, I suggest that a system of modern factories for the preparation of tea should be established in all the tea districts, so that the tea should be prepared by machinery instead of, as hitherto, by hand. Thus the cost of production can be greatly reduced and the quality improved. As the world's demand for tea is daily increasing and will be more so by a dry United States of America, a project to supply cheaper and better tea will surely be a profitable one.

Soya bean as a meat substitute was discovered by the Chinese and used by the Chinese and the Japanese as a staple food for many thousands of years. As meat shortage has been keenly felt in carnivorous countries at present, a solution must be found to relieve it. For this reason I suggest that in this International Development Scheme we should introduce this artificial meat, milk, butter and cheese to Europe and America, by establishing a system of soya bean factories in all the large cities of those countries, so as to provide cheap nitrogenous food to the western people. Modern factories should also be established in China to replace those old and expensive methods of production by hand, so as to procure better economic results as well as to produce better commodities.

PART II

The Clothing Industry

The principal materials for clothes are silk, linen, cotton, wool and animal skins. I shall accordingly deal with them under the following headings:

a. The Silk Industry.
b. The Linen Industry.
c. The Cotton Industry.
d. The Woolen Industry.
e. The Leather Industry.
f. The Manufacturing of Clothing Machinery.

A. THE SILK INDUSTRY

Silk is a Chinese discovery and was used as a material for clothes for many thousands of years before the Christian Era. It is one of the important national industries of China. Up to recent times, China was the only country that supplied silk to the world. But now this dominant trade has been taken away from China by Japan, Italy and France, because those countries have adopted scientific methods for silk culture and manufacture, while China still uses the same old methods of many thousand years ago. As the world's demand for silk is increasing daily, the improvement of the culture and manufacture of silk will be a very profitable undertaking. In this International Development Scheme, I suggest first that scientific bureaus be established in every silk district to give directions to the farmers and to provide healthy silk-worm eggs. These bureaus should be under central control. At the same time, they will act as collecting stations for cocoons so as to secure a fair price for the farmers. Secondly, silk filiatures with up-to-date machinery should be established in suitable districts to reel the silk for home as well as for foreign consumption. And lastly, modern factories should be put up for manufacturing silk for both home and foreign markets. All silk filiatures and factories should be under a single national control and will be financed with foreign capital and supervised by experts to secure the best economic results and to produce better and cheaper commodities.

B. THE COTTEN INDUSTRY

This is an old Chinese industry. In southern China there is produced a kind of very fine linen in the form of ramie, known as China-grass. This fiber if treated by modern methods and machinery becomes almost as fine and glossy as silk. But in China, so far as I know, there is not yet such new method and machinery for the manufacturing of this linen. The famous Chinese grass-cloth is manufactured by the old method of hand-looms. I propose that new methods and machinery be introduced into China by this International Development Organization to manufacture this linen. A system of modern factories should be established all over the ramie-producing districts in South China where raw materials and labor are obtainable.

C. THE COTTON INDUSTRY

Cotton is a foreign product which was introduced into China centuries ago. It became a very important Chinese industry during the hand-loom age. But after the import of foreign cotton goods into China, this native handicraft industry was gradually killed by the foreign trade. So, great quantities of raw cotton are exported and finished cotton goods are imported in large quantities into China. What an anomaly when we consider the enormous, cheap labor in China. However a few cotton mills have been started recently in treaty ports which have made enormous profits. It is reported that during the last two or three years most of the Shanghai cotton mills declared a dividend of

100 per cent and some even 200 per cent! The demand for cotton goods in China is very great but the supply falls short. It is necessary to put up more mills in China for cotton manufacturing. Therefore, I suggest in this International Development Scheme to put up a system of large cotton mills all over the cotton-producing districts under one central national control. Thus the best economic results will be obtained and cotton goods can be supplied to the people at a lower cost.

D. THE WOOLEN INDUSTRY

Although the whole of Northwestern China—about two-thirds of the entire country is a pastural land yet the woolen industry has never been developed. Every year, plenty of raw materials are exported from China on the one hand and plenty of finished woolen goods imported on the other. Judging by the import and export of the woolen trade the development of woolen industry in China will surely be a profitable business. I suggest that scientific methods be applied to the raising of sheep and to the treatment of wool so as to improve the quality and increase the quantity. Modern factories should be established all over northwestern China for manufacturing all kinds of finished woolen goods. Here we have the raw materials, cheap labor and unlimited market. What we want for the development of this industry is foreign capital and experts. This will be one of the most remunerative projects in our International Development Scheme, for the industry will be a new one and there will be no private competitors on the field.

E. THE LEATHER INDUSTRY

This will also be a new industry in China, despite the fact that there are a few tanneries in the treaty ports. The export of hides from and the import of leather goods into China are increasing every year. So, to establish a system of tanneries and factories for leather goods and foot-gear will be a lucrative undertaking.

F. THE MANUFACTURING OF CLOTHING MACHINERY

The machinery for the manufacturing of various kinds of clothing materials is in great demand in China. It is reported that the orders for cotton mill machinery have been filled up for the next three years from manufacturers in Europe and America. If China is developed according to my programs, the demand for machinery will be many times greater than at present and the supply in Europe and America will be too short to meet it. Therefore to establish factories for the manufacturing of clothing machinery is a necessary as well as a profitable undertaking. Such factories should be established in the neighborhood of iron and steel factories, so as to save expenses for transportation of heavy materials. What will be the capital for this undertaking should be decided by experts.

PART III

THE HOUSING INDUSTRY

Among the four hundred millions in China the poor still live in huts and hovels, and in caves in the loess region of north China while the middle and the rich classes live in temples. All the so-called houses in China, excepting a few after western style and those in treaty ports are built after the model of a temple. When a Chinese builds a house he has more regard for the dead than for the living. The first consideration of the owner is his ancestral shrine. This must be placed at the center of the house, and all the other parts must be complement and secondary to it. The house is planned not for comfort but for ceremonies, that is, for "the red and white affairs," as they are called in China. The "red affair" is the marriage or other felicitous celebrations of any member of the family, and the "white affair" is the funeral ceremonies. Besides the ancestral shrine there are the shrines of the various household gods. All these are of more importance than man and must be considered before him. There is not a home in old China that is planned for the comfort and convenience of man alone. So now when we plan the housing industry in China in our International Development Scheme, we must take the houses of the entire population of China into consideration. "To build houses for four hundred millions, it is impossible!" some may exclaim. This is the largest job ever conceived by man. But if China is going to give up her foolish traditions and useless habits and customs of the last three thousand years and begin to adopt modern civilization, as our industrial development scheme is going to introduce, the remodelling of all the houses according to modern comforts and conveniences is bound to come, either unconsciously by social evolution or consciously by artificial construction. The modern civilization so far attained by western nations is entirely an unconscious progress, for social and economic sciences are but recent discoveries. But henceforth all human progress will be more or less based upon knowledge, that is upon scientific planning. As we can forsee now, within half a century under our industrial development, the houses of all China will be renewed according to modern comfort and convenience. Is it not far better and cheaper to rebuild the houses of all China by a preconceived scientific plan than by none? I have no doubt that if we plan to build a thousand houses at one time it would be ten time cheaper than to plan and build one at a time, and the more we build the cheaper terms we would get. This is a positive economic law. The only danger in this is over-production. That is the only obstacle for all production on a large scale. Since the industrial revolution in Europe and America, every financial panic before the world war was caused by over-production. In the case of our housing industry in China, there are four hundred million customers. At least fifty million houses will be needed in the coming fifty years. Thus a million houses a year will be the normal demand of the country.

Houses are a great factor in civilization. They give men more enjoyment and happiness than food and clothes. More than half of the human industries are contributing to household needs. The housing industry will be the greatest undertaking of our International Development Scheme, and also will be the most profitable part of it. My object of the housing industry is to provide cheap houses to the masses. A ten thousand dollar house now built in the treaty port can be produced for less than a thousand dollars and yet a high margin of profit can be made. In order to accomplish this we have to produce transport, and distribute the materials for construction. After the house is finished, all household equipment must be furnished. Both of these will be comprised in the housing industry which I shall formulate as follows:

a. The Production and Transportation of Building Materials.

b. The Construction of Houses.

c. The Manufacturing of Furniture.

d. The Supply of Household Utilities.

A. THE PRODUCTION AND TRANSPORTATION OF BUILDING MATERIALS

The building materials are bricks, tiles, timber, skeleton iron, stone, cement and mortar. Each of these materials must be manufactured or cut out from raw materials. So kilns for the manufacture of tiles and bricks must be put up. Mills for timbers must be established, also factories for skeleton irons. Quarries must be opened and factories for cement and mortar must be started. All these establishments must be put up at suitable districts where materials and markets are near one another. All should be under one central control so as to regulate the output of each of these materials in proportion to the demand. After the materials are ready they must be transported to the places where they are wanted by special bottoms on waterways, and by special cars on railways so as to reduce the cost as low as possible. For this purpose special boats and cars must be built by the shipbuilding department and the car factory.

B. THE CONSTRUCTION OF HOUSES

The houses to be built in China will comprise public buildings and private residences. As the public buildings are to be built with public funds for public uses which will not be a profitable undertaking, a special Government Department should therefore be created to take charge. The houses that are to be built under this International Development Scheme will be private residences only with the object to provide cheap houses for the people, as well as to make profit for this International concern. The houses will be built on standardized types. In cities and towns the houses should be constructed on two lines: the single family and the group family houses. The former should again be subdivided into eight-roomed, ten-roomed and twelve-roomed houses, and the latter into ten-family, hundred-family and thousand-family houses, with four or six rooms for each family. In the country districts the houses should be classified according to the occupation of the people, and special annexes such as barns and dairies should be provided for the farmers. All houses should be designed and built according to the needs and comfort of man; so a special architectual department should be established to study the habits, occupations and needs of different people and make improvements from time to time. The construction should be performed as much as possible by labor-saving machinery so as to accelerate work and save expenses.

C. THE MANUFACTURING OF FURNITURE

As all houses in China should be remodelled all furniture should be replaced by up-to-date ones, which are made for the comforts and needs of man. Furniture of the following kinds should be manufactured: the library, the parlor, the bedroom, the kitchen, the bathroom and the toilet. Each kind should be manufactured in a special factory under the management of the International Development Organization.

D. THE SUPPLY OF HOUSEHOLD UTILITIES

The household utilities are water, light, heat, fuel and telephones. Except in treaty ports, there is no water-supply system in any of the cities and towns of China. Even many treaty ports possess none as yet. In all the large cities, the people obtain their water from rivers which at the same time act as sewage. The water supply of the large cities and towns in China is most unsanitary. (1) It is an urgent necessity that water supply systems should be installed in all cities and towns in China without delay. Therefore special factories for equipping the water system should be established in order to meet the needs. (2) Lighting plants should be installed in all the cities and towns in China. So factories for the manufacture of the machinery lighting plants should be established. (3) Modern heating plants should be installed in every household, using either electricity, gas, or steam. So the manufacturing of heating equipment is a necessity. Factories should be established for this purpose. (4) Cooking fuel is one of the most costly items in the daily needs of the Chinese people. In the country the people generally devote ten per cent of their working time to gathering firewoods. In town the people spend about twenty per cent of their living expenses for firewood alone. Thus this firewood question accumulates into a great national waste. The firewood and grass as a cooking fuel must be substituted by coal in the country districts, and by gas or electricity in towns and cities. In order to use coal gas and electricity, proper equipment must be provided. So factories for the manufacturing of coal gas, and electricity, stoves for every family must be established by this International Development Organization. (5) Telephones must also be supplied to every family in the cities as well as in the country. So factories for manufacturing the equipment must be put up in China, in order to render them as cheap as possible.

PART IV

THE MOTORING INDUSTRY

The Chinese are a stagnant race. From time immemorial a man is praised for staying at home and caring for his immediate surroundings only. Laotse—a contemporary of Confucius—says: "The good people are those who live in countries so near to each other that they can hear each other's cock crow and dog bark and yet they never have had intercourse with each other during their lifetime." This is often quoted as the Golden Age of the Chinese people. But in modern civilization the condition is entirely changed. Moving about occupies a great part of a man's life time. It is the movement of man that makes civilization progress. China, in order to catch up with modern civilization, must move. And the movement of the individual forms an important part of the national activity. A man must move whenever and wherever he pleases and ease and rapidity. However, China, at present, lacks the means of facility for individual movement, for all the old great highways were ruined and have disappeared, and the automobile has not yet been introduced into the interior of the country. The motor car, a recent invention, is a necessity for rapid movement. If we wish to move quickly and do more work, we must adopt the motor car as a vehicle. But before we can use the motor car, we have to build our roads. In the preliminary part of this International Development Scheme, I proposed to construct one million miles of roads. These should be apportioned according to the ratio of population in each district for construction. In the eighteen provinces of China Proper, there are nearly 2,000 hsiens. If all parts of China are to adopt the hsien administration, there will be nearly 4,000 hsiens in all. Thus the construction of roads for each hsien will be on an average of 250 miles. But some of the hsiens have more people and some have less. If we divide the million miles of roads by the four hundred million people, we shall have one mile to every four hundred. For four hundred people to build one mile of road is not a very difficult task to accomplish. If my scheme of making road-building as a condition for granting local autonomy is adopted by the nation, we shall see one million miles of road built in a very short time as if by a magic wand.

As soon as the people of China decide to build roads, this International Development Organization can begin to put up factories for manufacturing motor cars. First start on a small scale and gradually expand the plants to build more and more until they are sufficient to supply the needs of the four hundred million people. The cars should be manufactured to suit different purposes, such as the farmer's car, the artisan's car, the business man's car, the tourist's car, the truck car, etc. All these cars, if turned out on a large scale, can be made much cheaper than at present, so that everybody who wishes it, may have one.

Besides supplying cheap cars, we must also supply cheap fuel, otherwise the people will still be unable to use them. So the development of the oil fields in China should follow the motor car industry. This will be dealt with in more detail under the mining industry.

PART V

The Printing Industry

This industry provides man with intellectual food. It is a necessity of modern society, without which mankind cannot progress. All human activities are recorded, and all human knowledge is stored in printing. It is a great factor of civilization. The progress and civilization of different nations of the world are measured largely by the quantity of printed matter they turned out annually. China, though the nation that invented printing, is very backward in the development of its printing industry. In our International Development Scheme, the printing industry must also be given a place. If China is developed industrially according to the lines which I suggested, the demand for printed matter by the four hundred millions will be exceedingly great. In order to meet this demand efficiently, a system of large printing houses must be established in all large cities in the country, to undertake printing of all kinds from newspapers to encyclopædia. The best modern books on various subjects in different countries should be translated into Chinese and published in cheap edition form for the general public in China. All the publishing houses should be organized under one common management, so as to secure the best economic results.

In order to make printed matter cheap, other subsidiary industries must be developed at the same time. The most important of these is the paper industry. At present all the paper used by newspapers in China is imported. And the demand for paper is increasing every day. China has plenty of raw materials for making paper, such as the vast virgin forests of the northwestern part of the country, and the wild reeds of the Yangtze and its neighboring swamps which would furnish the best pulps. So, large plants for manufacturing papers should be put up in suitable locations. Besides the paper factories, ink factories, type foundries, printing machine factories, etc., should be established under a central management to produce everything that is needed in the printing industry.

PROGRAM VI

THE MINING INDUSTRY

Mining and farming are the two most important means of producing raw materials for industries. As farming is to produce food for man, so mining is to produce food for machinery. Machinery is the tree of modern industries, and the mining industry is the root of machinery. Thus, without the mining industry there would be no machinery, and without machinery there would be no modern industries which have revolutionized the economic conditions of mankind. The mining industry, after all, is the greatest factor of material civilization and economic progress. Although in the fifth part of the first program I suggested the development of the iron and coal fields in Chili and Shansi as an auxiliary project for the development of the Great Northern Port, still, a special program should be devoted to mining in general. The mineral lands of China belong to the state, and mining in China is still in its infancy. So to develop the mining industry from the outset as a state enterprise would be a sound economic measure. But mining in general is very risky and to enlist foreign capital in its development in a wholesale manner is unadvisable. Therefore, only such mining projects which are sure to be profitable will be brought under the International Development Scheme. I shall formulate this mining program as follows:

  I. The Mining of Iron.
  II. The Mining of Coal.
  III. The Mining of Oil.
  IV. The Mining of Copper.

V. The Working of Some Particular Mines.
VI. The Manufacture of Mining Machinery.
VII. The Establishment of Smelting Plants.

PART I

The Mining of Iron

Iron is the most important element in modern industries. Its deposits are found in great quantities in certain areas and be easily mined. The iron mines should be worked absolutely as a state property. Besides the Chili and Shansi iron mines, the other iron fields must also be developed. There are very rich deposits in the southwestern provinces, the Yangtze Valley and the northwestern provinces in China Proper. Sinkiang, Mongolia, Manchuria, Kokonor, and Tibet also possess large deposits of iron. We have the Han Yeh Ping Iron and Stell Works in the Yangtze Valley and the Pen Chi Hu Iron and Steel Works in South Manchuria, both of which are largely capitalized by Japan and are working very profitably lately. There should be similar works in the vicinity of Canton, the Great Southern Port, and also in Szechuen, and Yunnan, where iron and coal are found side by side. The iron deposits in Sinkiang, Kansu, Mongolia, etc., must also be developed one after the other, according to the needs of the locality. Iron and Steel Works must be put up in each of these regions to supply the local demand for manufactured iron. What amount of capital should be invested in these additional iron and steel works must be thoroughly investigated by experts. But I should say that a sum equal to or double the amount to be invested in the Chili and Shansi iron and steel works will not be too much, because of the great demand which will result in the development of China.

PART II

THE MINING OF COAL

China is known to be the country most rich in coal deposits, yet her coal fields are scarcely scratched. The output of coal in the United States is about six hundred million tons a year. If China is equally developed she should, according to the proportion of her population, have an output of four times as much coal as the United States. This will be the possibility of coal mining in China which the International Development Organization is to undertake. As coal deposits are found in great quantities in certain areas so its output can be estimated quite accurately beforehand. Thus, the risk is of no consideration and the profit is sure. But as coal is a necessity of civilized community and the sinews of modern industries, the principal object for mining should not be for profit alone, but for supplying the needs of mankind. After the payment of interest and capital of the foreign loans for its development, and the securing of high wages for the miners, the price of coal should be reduced as low as possible so as to meet the demands of the public as well as to give impetus to the development of various industries. I suggest that besides the mining of coal for the iron and steel works, a plan for producing two hundred million tons of coal a year for other uses should be formed at the start. Mines should be opened along the seaboard and navigable rivers. As Europe is now seeking coal from China this amount will not be over-production from the beginning. A few years later when the industries of China will be more developed more coal will be needed. How much capital will be required and what mines are to be worked, have to be submitted to scientific investigation under expert direction.

Besides coal mining, the coal products industry must be developed under the same management. This is a new industry without any competition and has an unlimited market in China. Great profits will be assured on the capital invested.

PART III

THE MINING OF OIL

It is well-known that the richest company in the world is the Standard Oil Company of New York, and that the richest man in the world is Rockefeller, organizer of this company. This proves that oil mining is a most profitable business. China is known to be a very rich oil-bearing country. Oil springs are found in the provinces of Szechuen, Kansu, Sinkiang, and Shensi. How vast is the underground reservoir of oil in China is not yet known. But the already known oil springs have never been worked and made use of, while the import of kerosene, gasoline, and crude oil from abroad is increasing every year. When China is developed as a motoring country, the use of gasoline will be increased a thousand-fold, then the supply from the foreign fields will not be able to meet the demands, as shortage of oil is already felt in Europe and America. The mining of oil in China will soon become a necessity. This enterprise should be taken up by the International Development Organization for the state. Production on a large scale should be started at once. Pipe line systems should be installed between oil districts and populous and industrial centers in the interior and also river and sea ports. What amount of capital should be invested in the project will have to be investigated by experts.

PART IV

THE MINING OF COPPER

The copper deposits, like iron ores, are found in great quantities in different places. So the quantity of ores in each mine can be accurately estimated before it is opened and its working generally runs no risk. Thus, the mining of copper should be taken up as a government enterprise, as was always the case in China, and financed and worked by the International Development Organization. The richest copper deposits in China are found along the border of Szechuen and Yunnan on the Yangtze River. The government copper mine in Chaotung, in the northeastern corner of Yunnan, has been working for many centuries. Cash, the standard currency of China, was made mostly of the copper from Yunnan province. The currency still absorbs an enormous quantity of copper. Owing to the difficulty of transporting the Yunnan copper, most of the metal for currency is being imported from foreign countries. Besides currency, copper is very commonly used for many other purposes and when the industries in China are developed the demand will increase a hundred times. So the demand for this metal will be very great in the market of China alone. I suggest that production on a large scale should be adopted and modern plants should be installed in copper mines. How much capital to be invested in this enterprise should be decided by experts after careful investigation.

PART V

The Working of Some Particular Mines

In regard to the mining of various kinds of metal, some particular mines should be taken up by the International Development Organization. There are many famous mines in China which have been worked for many centuries by hand, such as the Kochui tin mine in Yunnan, the Moho gold mine in Heilungkiang, and the Khotan jade mine in Sinkiang. All these mines are known to have very rich deposits,—the deeper the richer. Hitherto only the surface parts of those mines have been worked and the larger deposits are still untouched, owing to the lack of means of getting rid of the water. Some of the mines are still in the hands of the Government, while others have been given up to private concerns. If modern machinery is adopted the mines should revert to the Government so as to secure economy in working. Many discarded mines of this kind should be thoroughly investigated, and if found profitable, work should be resumed under the International Development Scheme. All future mining, other than government enterprise, should be leased to private concerns on contract, and when the term is up, the government has the option to take them over, if found profitable as a state property. Thus all profitable mines will be socialized in time and the profit will be equally shared by all the people in the country.

PART VI

The Manufacture of Mining Machinery

Most of the metal deposits of the earth are in small quantities and scattered far and wide in various places.

Most of the mining enterprises resemble farming in that it is more profitable to work by individuals and small parties. As such is the case, most of the mining enterprises have to be worked out by private concerns. In order to accelerate the development of mining, more liberal laws should be adopted; education and information should be given freely by experts employed by the state; and encouragement and financial assistance should be given by the state and private banks. The part that the International Development Organization should take in general mining enterprises is to manufacture all kinds of mining tools and machinery, and to supply them to the miners at low cost, either on cash or on credit. By distributing tools and machinery to the surplus workers in China, the mining industry would be developed by leaps and bounds. And the more the mining industry is developed the more will be the demand for tools and machinery. Thus the profits for the manufacturing concerns would be limitless, so to speak. Of course, the factories should be started on a small scale and be extended gradually according to the ratio of the development of the mining industry. I suggest that the first factory of this kind should be established at Canton, the seaport of the southwestern mining region, where raw materials and skilled labor can be easily obtained. The other factories should be established in Hankow and the Great Northern Port afterwards.

PART VII

The Establishment of Smelting Plants

Smelting plants for various kinds of metals should be put up in all mining districts to turn ore into metals. These smelting plants should be conducted under the cooperative system. At first, a reasonable price should be paid to the miner when the ore is collected. Afterwards, when the metal is sold, either at home or in foreign markets, the smelting works will take a share of the profit to cover the expenses, the interest, the sinking fund, etc. The surplus profit should be divided among the workers according to their wages, and among the capitalists according to the proportion of ore they contribute to the furnace. In this way we can encourage private mining enterprise which forms the root of other industries. All smelting works should be put up according to local needs and their scale should be determined by experts and managed under a central control.

CONCLUSION

In this International Development Scheme, I venture to present a practical solution for the three great world questions which are the International War, the Commercial War and the Class War. As it has been discovered by post-Darwin philosophers that the primary force of human evolution is coöperation and not struggle as that of the animal world, so the fighting nature, a residue of the animal instinct in man, must be eliminated from man, the sooner the better.

International war is nothing more than pure and simple organized robbery on a grand scale, which all right-minded people deplore. When the United States of America turned the recent European conflict into a world war by taking part in it, the American people to a man determined to make this war end war forever. And the hope of the peace-loving nations in the world was raised so high that we Chinese thought that the "Tatung" or the Great Harmony Age was at hand. But unfortunately, the United States has completely failed in peace, in spite of her great success in war. Thus, the world has been thrown back to the pre-war condition again. The scrambling for territories, the struggle for food, and the fighting for raw materials will begin anew. So instead of disarmament there is going to be a greater increase in the armies and navies of the once allied powers for the next war. China, the most rich and populous country in the world, will be the prize. Some years ago there was great inclination among the Powers to divide China and Imperial Russia actually took steps to colonize Manchuria. But the then chivalrous Japan went to war with Russia and thus saved China from partition.

Now the militaristic policy of Japan is to swallow China alone. So long as China is left to the tender mercy of the militaristic powers she must either succumb to partition by several powers or be swallowed up by one power.

However, the tide of the world seems to be turning. After centuries of sound slumber, the Chinese people at last are waking up and realizing that we must get up and follow in the world's progress. Now we are at the parting of the ways. Shall we organize for war or shall we organize for peace? Our militarists and reactionaries desire the former, and they are going to Japanize China, so that when the time comes they will start another Boxer Movement once more to defy the civilized world. But as the founder of the Chung Hwa Min Kuo—the Chinese Republic—I desire to have China organized for peace. I, therefore, begin to utilize my pen, which I hope will prove even mightier than the sword that I used to destroy the Manchu Dynasty, to write out these programs for organizing China for peace.

During the course of my writing, these programs have been published in various magazines and newspapers time after time and are being spread all over China. They are welcomed everywhere and by everyone in the country. So far there is not a word expressed in disfavor of my proposition. The only anxiety ever expressed regarding my scheme is where can we obtain such huge sums of money to carry out even a small part of this comprehensive project. Fortunately, however, soon after the preliminary part of my programs had been sent out to the different governments and the Peace Conference, a new Consortium was formed in Paris for the purpose of assisting China in developing her natural resources. This was initiated by the American

Government. Thus we need not fear the lack of capital to start work in our industrial development. If the Powers are sincere in their motive to cooperate for mutual benefit, then the military struggle for material gain in China could eventually be averted. For by cooperation, they can secure more benefits and advantages than by struggle. The Japanese militarists still think that war is the most profitable national pursuit, and their General Staff keeps on planning a war once in a decade. This Japanese illusion was encouraged and strengthened by the campaign of 1894 against China, a cheap and short one but rich in remuneration for Japan; also by the campaign of 1904 against Russia which was a great success to the Japanese, and its fruit of victory was no less in value; finally by the campaign of 1914 against Germany which formed her part in the world war Japan took. Although Japan took the smallest part in the world war and expended the least in men and money, yet the fruit of her victory was Shantung, a territory as large as Roumania before the war, with a population as numerous as that of France. With such crowning results in every war during the last thirty years no wonder the Japanese militarists think that the most profitable business in this world is War.

The effect of the last war in Europe proves, however, just the contrary. An aggresive Germany lost entirely her capital and interests, plus something more, while victorious France gained practically nothing. Since China is awake now, the next aggression from Japan will surely be met by a resolute resistance from the Chinese people. Even granted that Japan could conquer China, it would be an impossibility for Japan to govern China profitably for any period of time. The Japanese financiers possess better foresight than their militarists as was proved during the dispute of the Manchurian and the Mongolian reservations when the former prevailed over the latter thus causing the Japanese Government to give up her monopoly of these territories to the new Consortium, in order to cooperate with the other powers. We, the Chinese people, who desire to organize China for peace will welcome heartily this new Consortium provided it will carry out the principles which are outlined in these programs. Thus, cooperation of various nations can be secured and the military struggle for individual and national gain will cease forever.

Commercial war, or competition, is a struggle between the capitalists themselves. This war has no national distinction. It is fought just as furiously and mercilessly between countries as well as within the country. The method of fighting is to undersell each other, in order to exhaust the weaker rivals so that the victor may control the market alone and dictate terms to the consuming public as long as possible. The result of the commercial war is no less harmful and cruel to the vanquished foes than an armed conflict. This war has become more and more furious every day since the adoption of machinery for production. It was once thought by the economists of the Adam Smith school that competition was a beneficent factor and a sound economic system, but modern economists discovered that it is a very wasteful and ruinous system. As a matter of fact, modern economic tendencies work in a contrary direction, that is, towards concentration instead of competition. That is the reason why the trusts in America flourish in spite of the anti-trust law and the public opinion which aim at suppressing them. For trusts, by eliminating waste and cutting down expenses can produce much cheaper than individual producers. Whenever a trust enters into a certain field of industry, it always sweeps that field clean of rivals, by supplying cheap articles to the public. This would prove a blessing to the public but for the unfortunate fact that the trust is a private concern, and its object is to make as much profit as possible. As soon as all rivals are swept clean from the field of competition, the trust would raise the price of its articles as high as possible. Thus the public is oppressed by it. The trust is a result of economic evolution, therefore it is out of human power to suppress it. The proper remedy is to have it owned by all the people of the country. In my International Development Scheme, I intend to make all the national industries of China into a Great Trust owned by the Chinese people, and financed with international capital for mutual benefit. Thus once for all, commercial war will be done away with in the largest market of the world.

Class war is a struggle between labor and capital. The war is at present raging at its full height in all the highly developed industrial countries. Labor feels sure of its final victory while capitalists are determined to resist to the bitter end. When will it end and what will be the decision no one dares to predict. China, however, owing to the backwardness of her industrial development, which is a blessing in disguise, in this respect, has not yet entered into the class war. Our laboring class, commonly known as coolies, are living from hand to mouth and will therefore only be too glad to welcome any capitalist who would even put up a sweat shop to exploit them. The capitalist is a rare specimen in China and is only beginning to make his appearance in the treaty ports.

However, China must develop her industries by all means. Shall we follow the old path of western civilization? This old path resembles the sea route of Columbus' first trip to America. He set out from Europe by a southwesterly direction through the Canary Islands to San Salvador, in the Bahama Group. But nowadays navigators take a different direction to America and find that the destination can be reached by a distance many times shorter. The path of western civilization was an unknown one and those who went before groped in the dark as Columbus did on his first voyage to America. As a late comer, China can greatly profit in covering the space by following the direction already charted by western pioneers. Thus we can foresee that the final goal of the westward-ho in the Atlantic is not India but the New World. So is the case in the economic ocean. The goal of material civilization is not private profit but public profit. And the shortest route to it is not competition but co-operation. In my International Development Scheme, I propose that the profits of this industrial development go first to pay the interest and principal of foreign capital invested in it; second to give high wages to labor; and third to improve or extend the machinery of production. Besides these provisions the rest of the profit should go to the public in the form of reduced prices in all commodities and public services. Thus, all will enjoy, in the same degree, the fruits of modern civilization. This industrial development scheme which is roughly sketched in the above six programs is a part of my general plan for constructing a New China. In a nutshell, it is my idea to make capitalism create socialism in China so that these two economic forces of human evolution will work side by side in future civilization.

APPENDIX I

PRELIMINARY AGREEMENT PROVIDING FOR THE FINANCING AND CONSTRUCTION OF THE RAILWAY FROM CANTON TO CHUNGKING WITH EXTENSION TO LANCHOW

This Agreement is made at Shanghai on the fourth day of the seventh month of the second year of the Republic of China being the fourth day of July, 1913, and the contracting parties are: The Chinese National Railway Corporation (hereinafter termed "the Corporation") duly authorized in virtue of the Presidential Mandate of the ninth day of the ninth month of the Republic of China being the ninth day of September, 1912, and in virtue of the Charter of the Corporation duly promulgated by a Presidential Mandate of the thirty-first day of the third month of the second year of the Republic of China being the thirty-first day of March, 1913, on the one part and Messrs. Pauling and Company, Limited, of 26 Victoria Street, London, S. W. (hereinafter termed "the Contractors") on the other part.

Now IT IS HEREBY AGREED by and between the parties hereto as follows:

ARTICLE I

The Contractors, or their Assigns, agree to issue on behalf of the Government of the Republic of China a sterling Loan, bearing interest at the rate of five per cent per annum, (hereinafter referred to as "the Loan") for such an amount as may be mutually estimated to be necessary for the completion of the Railway from Canton to Chungking.

The Loan shall be of the date on which the first series of Bonds are issued and shall be called "The Chinese National Railways Government five per cent Gold Loan of 1912 for the Canton Chungking Railway."

ARTICLE II

The proceeds of the Loan are designed for the construction and equipment of the Railway from Canton to Chungking (hereinafter called "the Railway") and for all necessary expenditure appertaining thereto as may be arranged in the Detailed Agreement, referred to in Article 17.

ARTICLE III

The payment of the interest and the redemption of the Capital of the Loan are guaranteed by the Government of the Republic of China and by a special lien upon the Canton Chungking Railway.

This special lien constitutes a first mortgage in favour of the Contractors, acting on behalf of the Bondholders, upon the Railway itself, as and when constructed, and on the revenue of all descriptions derivable therefrom, and upon all materials, rolling stock and buildings of every description purchased or to be purchased for the Railway.

Should there be default in payments on the dates fixed of all or part of the half yearly interest or amortization payments, the Contractors shall have the right to exercise on behalf of the Bondholders all the rights of action which accrue to them from the special mortgage.

ARTICLE IV

During the time of construction of the Railway the interest on the Bonds and on any advances made by the Contractors shall be paid from the proceeds of the Loan. The accruing interest from any proceeds of the Loan not used during the period of construction, and the earnings derived by the Corporation from the working of any sections of the Railway as they are built, are to be used to make up the amount required for the payment of the said interest, and if any deficiency remains it is to be met from the proceeds of the Loan.

When the construction of the Railway is wholly completed, the interest on the Bonds is to be paid from the income or earnings of the Railway received by the Corporation, in such manner and on such dates as may be provided for in the Detailed Agreement provided for in Article 17 of this Agreement.

If, at any time, the earnings of the Railway, together with the funds available from the proceeds of the Loan, are not sufficient to meet the interest on the Bonds and the repayment of the capital in accordance with the Amortization Schedule to be attached to the Detailed Agreement, the Government of the Republic of China, in approving of this Agreement, unconditionally undertakes and promises to pay the principal of the Loan and the interest of the Loan on the due dates to be fixed therefore in the Detailed Agreement provided for in Article 17 of this Agreement.

ARTICLE V

The bonds shall be Bonds of the Government of the Republic of China.

ARTICLE VI

The Loan shall be issued to the public in two or more series of Bonds, the first issue to be made to the amount of from one to two million pounds sterling as soon as possible after the signature of the Detailed Agreement referred to in Article 17 of this Agreement. The issue price of the Bonds shall be fixed by the Corporation and the Contractors sometime before the issue, taking the last price of similar Bonds as a basis for fixing the market price. The price payable to the Corporation shall be the actual rate of issue to the public less a sufficient amount to cover the cost of stamps on the Bonds in the various countries of issue, provided always that at least fifty per cent of the Bonds shall be issued in England, plus floatation charges of four per cent retainable by the Contractors (that is to say, a charge of four pounds for every one hundred pound Bond issued).

After the Detailed Agreement referred to in Article 17 is settled, and pending the issue of the Loan, the Contractors shall deposit the sum of fifty thousand pounds with the issuing Bank to the Canton Chungking Railway account, and this amount can be drawn on by the Corporation for survey and other necessary expenses authorized by the Managing Director against certificates signed by the Chief Accountant and Chief Engineer. This sum of fifty thousand pounds shall bear interest at the rate of five per cent per annum and shall be refunded out of the proceeds of the Loan.

ARTICLE VII

The proceeds of the Loan shall be deposited with the issuing Bank, to be nominated and guaranteed by the Contractors, to the credit of a Canton Chungking Railway Account on such terms as may be mutually arranged in the Detailed Agreement referred to in Article 17.

When the work of construction is ready to begin a sum equal to the estimated expenditure in China for six months shall be transferred to a Bank in China to be mutually agreed upon and there placed to the credit of a Canton Chungking Railway Account to be operated upon by the Corporation under certificates signed by the Chief Accountant and the Chief Engineer. This amount of estimated expenditure for six months shall be maintained by subsequent monthly transfers so that, as far as possible, there shall always be six months estimated expenditure in China on deposit in a Bank in China to be mutually agreed upon.

ARTICLE VIII

Immediately after the signing of the Detailed Agreement, the Corporation will establish a Head Office at Canton for the Canton Chungking Railway. This Office will be under the direction of a Chinese Managing Director to be appointed by the Corporation, with whom will be associated a British Engineer-in-Chief and a British Firm of Public Accountants, of recognized standing, whose representative shall be Chief Accountant (hereinafter called "the Chief Accountant"). These British Employes shall be nominated by the Corporation and the Contractors, jointly, and shall be appointed by the Corporation. Their dismissal shall take place, only, with the joint approval of the Corporation and the Contractors.

It is understood that the duties to be performed by these employes are intended to promote the mutual interests of the Corporation and the Bondholders respectively, and it is therefore agreed that all cases of difference arising therefrom shall be referred for amicable adjustment between the Corporation and the Representative of the Contractors. The salaries and other terms of Agreement of the Engineer-in-Chief and the Chief Accountant shall be arranged between the Corporation and the Contractors; and the amount of their salaries, etc., shall be paid out of the general accounts of the Railway.

For all important technical appointments for the operation of the Railway, Europeans of experience and ability shall be engaged and wherever competent Chinese are available, they shall be employed. All such appointments shall be made, and their functions defined, by the Managing Director and the Engineer-in-Chief in consultation, and shall be submitted for the approval of the Corporation; similar procedure shall be followed in the case of Europeans employed in the Chief Accountant's department. In the event of the misconduct, or the incompetency of these European employes, their services may be dispensed with by the Managing Director, after consulation with the Engineer-in-Chief, and subject to the sanction of the Corporation. The form of Agreements made with these European Employes shall conform to the usual practice.

APPENDIX I

The accounts of the receipts and the disbursements of the Railway's construction and operation, shall be in Chinese and English in the department of the Chief Accountant, whose duty it shall be to organize and supervise the same, and to report thereon for the information of the Corporation through the Managing Director, and of the Contractors as representing the Bondholders. All receipts and payments shall be certified by the Chief Accountant and authorized by the Managing Director.

For the general technical staff of the Railway, after completion of construction, the necessary arrangements shall be made by the Managing Director in consultation with the Engineer-in-Chief, and reported to the Corporation in due course.

The duties of the Engineer-in-Chief shall consist in the efficient and economical maintenance of the Railway, and the general supervision thereof in consultation with the Managing Director. The duties of the Chief Engineer during construction shall be set forth in the Detailed Agreement, referred to in Article 17 of this Agreement.

The Engineer-in-Chief shall always give courteous consideration to the wishes and instructions of the Corporation, whether conveyed directly or through the Managing Director, and shall always comply therewith, having at the same time due regard to the efficient construction and maintenance of the Railway.

A school for the education of Chinese in Railway matters shall be established by the Managing Director subject to the approval of the Corporation.

ARTICLE IX

The Contractors shall construct and equip the Railway and shall receive as remuneration a sum equal to seven per cent on the actual cost of the construction and equipment of the Railway. The term "Equipment" shall be held to include in its meaning all requirements necessary for the operation of the Railway and shall therefore include Rolling Stock and Locomotives sufficient for operation.

It is clearly understood that the term "Equipment" does not include any purchases made for the Railway after it has been completely constructed and equipped and handed over ready for operation.

It is further clearly understood that the cost of land purchased for the Railway, the salaries of the Managing Director, Chief Accountants, Chief Engineer, and the cost of their offices and staff shall not be included in the meaning of the terms "construction and equipment."

The Contractors shall have the option of constructing on the same terms the proposed extension of the Railway to Lanchow in the Province of Kansu, or a Railway of similar milage in some other part of China to be mutually agreed upon, and this option shall be for seven years from the commencement of construction.

All other arrangements in connection with the construction and equipment of the Railway shall be settled in the Detailed Agreement referred to in Article 17.

ARTICLE X

All land that may be required along the whole course of the Railway within survey limits, and for the necessary sidings, stations, repairing shops and car sheds, to be provided for in accordance with the detailed plans, shall be acquired by the Corporation at the actual cost of the land, and shall be paid for out of the proceeds of the Loan.

ARTICLE XI

The Contractors shall hand over to the Corporation each section of the Railway, when completed, for operation in accordance with the provisions of the Detailed Agreement.

ARTICLE XII

The Contractors shall be appointed Trustees for the Bondholders and shall receive such remuneration as may be fixed in the Detailed Agreement.

ARTICLE XIII

The Government of the Republic of China, whenever necessary, will provide protection for the Railway while under construction or when in operation, and all the properties of the Railway as well as Chinese and foreigners employed thereon, are to enjoy protection from the local Officials.

The Railway may maintain a force of Chinese Police with Chinese officers, their wages and maintenance to be wholly defrayed as part of the cost of the construction and maintenance of the Railway. In the event of the Railway requiring further protection by the military forces of the Government, the same shall be duly applied for by the

Head Office and promptly afforded, it being understood that such military forces shall be maintained at the expense of the Government.

ARTICLE XIV

All materials of any kind that are required for the construction and working of the Railway, whether imported from abroad or from the Provinces to the scene of work, shall be exempted from Likin or other duties so long as such exemption remains in force in respect of other Chinese Railways. The Bonds of the Loan, together with their coupons and the income of the Railway shall be free from imposts of any kind by the Government of the Republic of China.

ARTICLE XV

With a view to encouraging Chinese industries, Chinese materials are to be preferred, provided price and quality are suitable.

At equal rates and qualities, goods of British manufacture shall be given preference over other goods of foreign origin.

ARTICLE XVI

The Contractors may, with the approval of the Corporation, and subject to all their obligations, transfer or delegate all or any of their rights, powers and discretions, to their successors or assigns.

APPENDIX I

ARTICLE XVII

As soon as this Preliminary Agreement is signed it shall be forwarded to the Government of the Republic of China for approval. When it has met with the approval of the Government of the Republic of China, a necessary Detailed Agreement shall be made embodying the principles of this Agreement with such amplifications and additions as may be mutually agreed upon between the parties hereto.

ARTICLE XVIII

On its approval of this Agreement, and acceptance of the obligations set forth herein, the Government of the Republic of China shall officially notify the British Minister at Peking of the fact, and this approval shall be taken as covering the Detailed Agreement referred to in Article 17.

ARTICLE XIX

This Agreement is executed in quadruplicate in English and Chinese, one copy to be retained by the Corporation, one to be forwarded to the Government of the Republic of China, one to be forwarded to the British Minister at Peking, and one to be retained by the Contractors, and should any doubt arise as to the interpretation of the Agreement the English text shall be accepted as the standard.

Signed at Shanghai by the contracting parties on this fourth day of the seventh month of the second year of the Republic of China being the fourth day of July nineteen hundred and thirteen.

APPENDIX II

Legation of the United States of America

Peking, March 17, 1919.

Dr. Sun Yat-sen,
29 Rue Molière,
Shanghai, Kiangsu.

Dear Dr. Sun:

I have read with great interest your sketch project for the international development of China as embodied in your letter of February first to me. I congratulate you upon the broad and statesmanlike attitude with which you treat this very important subject. Your suggestion of united international participation in the development of China's resources deserves the support of all friends of China. It would be unfortunate indeed if the old regime of spheres of influence, struggles for concessions and activities flavoring of selfish exploitation should not, with the conclusion of the war, be relegated to the past. You are right in recognizing the necessity of a substitute for the old order and your proposal of a unified policy under international organization with Chinese participation for the larger development in China, naturally assuming that the inalienable rights of the Chinese people are to be amply safeguarded, meets this demand admirably.

We are hopeful that conditions in China may become such that the Chinese people themselves may be encouraged to put their money into productive enterprise and participate in the larger developments. We are hopeful

APPENDIX II

that the day is not far distant when the Chinese Government may be able actively to interest itself in the encouragement of native industry to the end that native capital of which there is a very considerable quantity, may be induced to lend itself to productive enterprises, because of a confidence in constructive policy on the part of the government.

If you will permit a suggestion, I would be inclined to reduce your admirable program to one which would be in closer keeping with the limits of the present world's resources in capital. As we all know devastated Europe is calling for capital for rehabilitation and other nations want capital for development programs of considerable proportions. Thus it would seem that China's program of development must of necessity take cognizance of her most immediate and most pressing needs. We are all united in that transportation occupies a prominent place in such a program. 50,000 miles of railway and 100,000 miles of good roads would seem to be sufficient to engage our attention for any plans for the immediate future. This would allow ample opportunity to penetrate the great rich unoccupied regions in the North and West, which should be opened to colonization and development as soon as possible in order to relieve the economic pressure of over population in sections along the coasts and waterways, and to accord opportunities to bring the rich regions of West China into contact with the trade of the rest of China and the world at large.

Along with transportation, China needs to develop its resources in iron and coal, the two great essentials to modern industrialism. Arrangements should be made whereby foreign capital can come to China's assistance in these two important industries, but care should be exercised so as to preserve to China the iron and coal necessary for its own uses, and prevent China's steel industry being mortgaged to foreign interests, in a way so as to jeopardize China's future in this important industry.

The reform of the currency and reforms in internal tax administrations are questions of immediate importance to China's economic and industrial development.

One of the greatest fields of potentiality in the immediate demands of the New China, is agriculture. The country depends in its final analysis upon the prosperity of its agriculture. At present probably as much as 80% of China's population is agricultural. China's greatest problem is the proper feeding and clothing of its vast population. Improved conditions in agriculture, opening of new lands to cultivation, irrigation and conservancy works, the encouragement of the cattle and sheep industries, the development of the cotton industry and the improvement of tea, silk and the seed crops of China, are timely subjects in any program of developments. There is a vast work to be done in agriculture in China, which will lead to prosperity generally, and make possible developments with native capital in other fields of activity, whereas if agricultural improvements are neglected, it will be difficult to insure prosperity in other directions.

Thus for the present, I hope the main thought may be centered on improvements in transportation, in currency and tax administrations, in the development of coal and iron industries, and in agriculture. Many of the suggested activities included in your very extensive program will follow as a corollary to the above.

In thinking of all these developments, I believe that we should always give thought to the fact that we are not dealing with a new country but with one in which social arrangements are exceedingly intricate and in which a long-tested system of agricultural and industrial organization exists. It is to my mind most important that the transition to new methods of industry and labor should not be sudden but that the old abilities and values should be gradually transmuted. It is important that the artistic ability existing in the silk and porcelain manufacture, etc. should be maintained and fostered, and not superseded by cheaper processes. It is also highly important that no export of food should be permitted, except as to clearly ascertained surpluses of production. It would produce enormous suffering were the food prices in China suddenly to be raised to the world market level. The one factor in modern organization which the Chinese must learn better to understand is the corporation, and the fiduciary relationship which the officers of the corporation ought to occupy with respect to the stockholders. If the Chinese cannot learn to use the corporation properly, the organization of the national credit cannot be effected. Here, too, it is necessary that the capital of personal honesty which was accumulated under the old system should not be lost but transferred to the new methods of doing business. So at every point where we are planning for a better and more efficient organization, it seems necessary to hold on to the values created in the past and not to disturb the entire balance of society by too sudden changes.

I wish again to congratulate you upon the statesman-like view with which you consider the whole question of the development of your country, and the very timely suggestions you have to make in regard to a united policy of international participation in these developments. I am glad to note that the minds of the leaders among the Chinese people today are being centered more and more upon the constructive needs of the country and efforts are being made to meet these needs, in full appreciation of China's relations with the people of other nations, to the end that China's developments in the future may work in harmony with the world developments generally.

I should be glad to hear from you further and more in detail concerning development plans.

Believe me, with the highest regard,
Sincerely yours,
(Signed)
Paul S. Reinsch.

APPENDIX III

DEPARTMENT OF COMMERCE
Office of the Secretary
Washington

May 12, 1919.

Hon. Sun Yat-sen,
29 Rue Molière,
Shanghai, China.

Your Excellency:

I have read with the greatest interest the project for the International Development of China enclosed in your letter of March 17th, and agree with you that the economic development of China would be of the greatest advantage, not only to China, but to the whole of mankind.

The plans you propose, however, are so complex and extensive that it will take many years to work them out in detail. You doubtless are fully aware that it would take billions of dollars to carry out even a small portion of your proposals and that most of them would not be able to pay interest charges and expenses of operation for some years. The first question to be decided, therefore, is how the interest charges on the necessary loans could be met. The revenues of the Chinese Republic are already too heavily burdened with the interest charges on existing Government loans to warrant further charges, and hence it would seem necessary for the present to limit the projects for development to those which seem sufficiently remunerative to attract private capital. The government of the United States has consistently endeavored to manifest its disinterested friendship for the people of China and will undoubtedly cooperate in every proper way in proposals to advance their best interests.

Please accept my thanks for your kindness in submitting your proposals.

Respectfully,
(Signed)
WILLIAM C. REDFIELD,
Secretary.

APPENDIX IV

Il Ministro Della Guerra

Rome, 17 Maggio, 1919.

Most Honorable
Sun Yat-sen,
29 Rue Moliere,
Shanghai, China.

Honorable Sir:

I thank you for having so kindly communicated to me the interesting project regarding how to employ through an International Organization the exuberant industrial activities created by the war, in order to exploit the great hidden riches of China.

Though aware of the practical difficulties which present themselves in the accomplishment of this project, it meets with my utmost appreciation, I assure you, for the modern spirit by which it is animated and for the depth of its conception.

Accept my best wishes for complete success, in the advantage of your noble country and for the interest of humanity.

Believe Me,

Faithfully yours,
(Signed)

General Caviglia.

APPENDIX V

Peking, June 17, 1919.

Hon. Sun Yat-sen,
Shanghai.

Dear Sir:

Permit me as a professional railway man to express my pleasure with your article appearing in the Far Eastern Review for June.

I will not at this time express approval or disapproval of the route which you have chosen but the idea of a line to connect up the great agricultural interior with the densely populated coast appeals to me strongly. I feel that you are making a definite contribution to railway economic theory in this respect, whereas the line itself would relieve congestion, open up a production area which would lower food costs, furnish employment to large numbers of soldiers to be disbanded, and put in circulation a large amount of hard money which would go far to correct the currency situation.

I am especially pleased to have your article appear at this time for I had already written one at the request of the publishers of the forthcoming "Trans-Pacific" magazine in which I touched upon the same line of thought. This will not appear until July and your opinions will have done much to prepare the minds of sceptics upon the subject by that time.

I trust that this intrusion of an entire stranger may be pardoned, and that you will continue to support the

APPENDIX V

thought which you have so ably presented.

>Very truly yours,
>(Signed)
>J. E. BAKER.

APPENDIX VI

3, Piazza Del Popolo
Roma

August 30, 1919.

Dr. Sun Yat-sen,
29 Rue Moliére,
Shanghai, China.

My Dear Dr. Sun Yat-sen:

I thank you for your very kind letter of June 19th which has just been forwarded to me from my office in Rome, also for your kindness in sending me your splendid project "To assist the Re-adjustment of Post-bellum Industries," and the program for "The International Development of China."

I assure you I read your proposals and studied the maps in connection with your able and logical argument with the deepest interest. And I beg you to accept my hearty congratulations.

I am entirely convinced that your noble *ideals will be* realised, not only for the benefit of China and the welfare of your own people, but for the benefit and prosperity of the whole human race.

The Nations cannot continue to deny in the future as they have in the past, the unlimited natural resources of your rich fertile country, in foods, minerals, coal and iron, etc.; and your plans for development and activity, as well as your methods of communication for expanding and cul-

APPENDIX VI

tivating almost untouched miles of virgin soil, and bringing these products to the doors of the "World Market" by a practical and economic plan, scientifically studied out, places you at once among the very rare few unselfish humanitarian benefactors, and reveals so clearly your profound international sympathies.

The development of China's natural resources will give a new impetus and vitality to industry and commerce in your country and will not only be of incalculable benefit to your own people, but offer undeniable and unlimited advantages to all people in all nations. Therefore Governments and foreign financiers should not hesitate in giving your plans their most careful consideration and support, and come to your assistance in the realisation of your grand humanitarian project.

The construction of a great "Northern Port" on the Gulf of Pechili, and the building of a system of railways from this great Northern Port to the northwestern extremity of China, as well as the construction of canals to connect the inland waterways systems of North and Central China with the great "Northern Port," and the development of coal and iron fields in Shansi which would necessitate the construction of iron and steel works would not only offer employment to millions of your country people, but would open wider, and advantageously, the doors of thousands of well organised industries in many nations.

It is very encouraging to me, dear Dr. Sun Yat-sen, to know that you look upon my plans of an "International World Centre of Communication" with favor, and that you will further the idea among your countrymen by writing about it in your magazine "The Construction."

This city, erected upon neutral grounds would offer at once the practical framework for the essential needs of a League of Nations and could become its dignified "Administrative Centre" crowned by an International Court of Justice.

I have presented the plans and proposals of this World Centre to the Rulers and governments of all nations, and hope to be able to go to Washington in October to exhibit the large original drawings and personally explain the project from a practical and economic point of view before the foreign delegates who may meet there to assist in the formation of a League of Nations, and I have written to President Wilson, who after receiving the volumes containing the proposals and plans, wrote that "he valued them very highly."

I hope that in the very near future this International World Centre of communication may become a reality. It would be the means of clearly defining and bringing into focus the highest natural products as well as the most important industrial achievements of all countries. The accomplishment would be one of the first definite steps toward more friendly social and economic relations, and the practicability of establishing such cooperation cannot be disputed.

This City of Peace should rise and stand as an International Monument, erected by international contribution to commemorate the heroic struggle and noble sacrifice of millions who gave their lives on the battle fields, in the air and on the sea, that justice should triumph and open

...e ways for humanity to progress in peace, and free from ...nny in the future.

With the assurance, dear Dr. Sun Yat-sen, of my most ...und sympathies for your noble project, and with my ... gratitude for your keen interest in my plans,

I beg to remain, with high esteem

Faithfully yours,
(Signed)

HENDRICK CHRISTIAN ANDERSEN.